Life at 70

PEDAL
TO THE
METAL

SANFORD J. HOROWITZ

Edited by Cindy Davis and Anton Horowitz
Cover design by Grady Earls
Interior artwork by Skye Horowitz
Interior design by Toni Kerr

Manufactured in the United States of America
First Edition October 2018

Deep appreciation to my senior friends at the "round table" at Coffee Traders, in Whitefish, Montana. I won't include their names because I just don't know who's name to write down first and in what order and anyway they know who they are.

I don't believe you could put together a more diverse group of mostly men, and yet, they have established a bond of friendship and genuine caring for each other that rivals any such group in any great novel. I am truly humbled they were gracious enough to allow me to share their honored company. Enough said... except, I love you guys.

God does not ask
you to be perfect,
only that you become
a little better
each and every day.

Introduction

Being an elder has inherent value in all cultures. It has been proven over man's entire history that to live life properly, it is a wise decision to allow this added voice of experience into our lives.

Elders, or seniors, have been a cornerstone of the collective whole of humanity, adding the elements of wisdom, experience, and having the perspective of the big picture, a proven tool of avoiding many of life's difficult moments and mistakes.

I'm not saying that because we have aged, it has given us complete-knowing. The humble part of us knows better. And quite honestly, if that was true, there would be no need for me to write this book because imparting spiritual wisdom to my fellow seniors is a big part of what this book is about.

The other reason for writing this book is to encourage my fellow elders to stay engaged because it is my firm belief that to eliminate our voices would greatly diminish the health of humanity at large. I believe it is our inherent right for our generation to regain our voices and to bring back our influence as God designed it. Whether in the family, running a company, or running a country, and in some cases running the known world, the elder's voice has proven to serve as a reliable source for decision-making and moving humanity forward.

I have looked at our own generation of elders and marveled at their accomplishments. We have produced lasting music, art, architecture, science breakthroughs, spiritual breakthroughs, movies, and on and on. There is no doubt that we are special in many, many ways.

The other observations I've made are that many seniors have much more to give.

I hope this book will further inspire those seniors to play a more active role in our society as God intended. It is also a reminder for all seniors to be more of a collective voice. I believe it is time to reclaim God's plan of having our voice heard again and Lord knows, our planet needs it.

And on that note, if one is going to be a positive influence, it is best to be prepared. So, with that in mind, I have decided to pass on some spiritual wisdom I've acquired along the way. One can assume that by the time we become seniors, acquiring spiritual wisdom is a forgone conclusion. Unfortunately, that's not always the case.

CHAPTER 1

To Inspire

Some may wonder, what qualifications that I, Sanford J Horowitz possess to open my mouth about anything. Well, if you're looking for a long list of academic credentials, I'll come up way short. But, as many of us know by now, credentials don't always solve the problem. After all, it is not uncommon for regular people who rise from the crowd to say, "Hey, I think I've discovered a way to help out." And guess what—the good ones get to write book #2.

All I know is that I was "inspired" to write my words to you and that's how this all got started. From almost the very beginning of my conscious memory, the question that always popped into my head was, what is the meaning to all this, and I mean, *All of this*! And me being a kid, that question became my *inspiration* to reach out and explore life any way I could.

There have been many ups and downs in my life with only shallow answers to offer. However, if you like what I have to say, then I will say God had a hand in this process. Either way, in fact, God had his hand in this.

All humans are connected by the truth. I am told we are born with this information, but it just needs to be rediscovered. Why? Because a fundamental rule for personal growth is that we need to re-learn it, re-earn it for each life time, in the form of knowledge and wisdom.

Another secret about "knowledge" I learned, is that its main purpose is to *inspire*. How interesting I thought. But because it actually made sense, I embraced it and soon it became my engine that was behind this journey.

Driven by this desire to know more about how it all works became more and more fascinating to me. The problem of course, what road should I drive down as my source for answers? I knew that question laying in front of me would become one of those defining moments, and that it would determine my true life's path, which ultimately became the world of "spirituality".

So, how did I choose the world of spirituality? Honestly, when I thought back to that decision, it was to a consistent feeling I got way back in college. Somehow, I was drawn to books with a mystical and spiritual point of view. Classics like, *Sid Arthur*, and authors like Dostoevsky. It just made a strong impact on me. It was a truth that I connected to. So, to me, that was the answer to my question. Spiritual truths were where I was going. Its practical rewards were so concrete and something I could easily test in real life situations. Nothing was hypothetical because the results appeared right in front of my eyes and my life became better and better. So, I turned the key, and there I went, pedal to the metal!

Being inspired by my new spiritual findings became like an addiction. Almost every answer or secret I uncovered, inspired me to the next secret, and the next answer.

So, how does this relate to you, the reader? Being inspired is simply a mindset to seek knowledge. Its benefits have been the best feeling and it can be yours as well.

After years of learning and finding new truths, I came to understand the power and benefits of sharing what I have discovered. I learned that sharing is the most fundamental gift from God and his most defining quality.

Inspiration is a gift as well. After all, this is the purpose of this chapter! But this does not come easy. I can give all of you answers to the universe but until you put in the effort, to truly comprehend the information and put it to use, what's the point?

Yes, all this will take work on your part but at least you will be well armed like never before. I even guarantee satisfactory results will follow, even amazing results.

All the knowledge every one of you have, come with certain responsibilities given to us, divinely. It's part of your assets that you have already acquired that may, in fact, far exceed what you have in your bank and then some. So, don't ever diminish it or write it off. It is those assets that ONLY seniors possess. These are your assets, once you honestly see them as assets, this will fuel you and inspire you to know more.

For reasons I will reveal later, society is attempting to down grade our role in the world, especially here in the US. And the truth is, they have done this because they fear us and fear our voice.

Our planet needs all of you. Look around. Most of

us are of this special generation of the sixties. This is no accident of who we are and what we have collectively accomplished. What I believe is that we have yet another vision for the future generation. And we need to make it happen. Our planet is a mess, relying only on technology to solve problems.

What came to me after much thought, was that we are the only generation qualified to look to the past, present, and into the future, for sound solutions. Who else has that unique perspective? Technology, like computers, requires content. Our voices need to be a part of that content. We are really a gift to society, not the burden that is often projected. Our voice needs to be something that is heard, proud, and respected.

The other morning, I had a vision of standing on a mountaintop, arms spread, looking over this amazing view of other snowcapped mountains as far as the eye could see. Man, was I feeling inspired! The image that came over me, I later realized, wasn't only about me but was about all of us, collectively, looking out, imagining what we can accomplish. Sounds outrageous but isn't this what we have done? Haven't we all climbed this mountain of life, more treacherous than the real thing?

I'm not saying we have only done stupendous feats or anything like that because life is not like that. A person could have accumulated masses of wealth and fail as a father, mother, son or daughter, husband or wife. And a person could have lived a simple, modest life and raised amazing children. It's all relative. Hopefully we have all learned that by now. So, is all of us standing on top of that mountain so far-fetched? Look back. Appreciate, and thank God for everything we might have done, big or small. It will inspire you.

Anyone who is considered a senior, or elder, has earned that space where I stood—one way or another. As a student of history, how often have I read that what became the difference between winning and losing was often some inconsequential, minor mistake or tiny event that turned the tide of a battle, war, or even the direction of mankind itself. In short, it is not up to us to judge other people's merits or life history. Yes, we all deserved a respected space among the society we helped to build.

It is my belief that each one of us is here on earth for a reason. Since I believe in reincarnation, that reason may be very complex. But since my belief system also believes that God is the mastermind of it all, we may not truly understand our mission here on earth right away. It can take years—many years. Which leads me to the next point.

Why did God create us older people? Do you think we came about without a reason, or just to collect social security?

For most of civilization, "the elders" have been revered, but why? Why did God divide us by ages—babies, tots, kids, teens, 20's, 30's, 40's, 50's, 60's, 70's and beyond and put us at the top? Remember, God never does anything without a reason. In fact, God had to be inspired himself when he created seniors. Someone with a lifetime of knowledge to add to the mix seems brilliant to me.

So, maybe it's time we turn another page, like back to the future, to a system God created, instead of one created by, who knows? I believe we elders need to step forward in this society and reclaim our place. We must redefine our place and our voices and get back in the game. I know our generation and I am absolutely convinced we have what it takes. However, we must reclaim it in a new and creative way. The only decision we need to make—and I mean collectively—is whether to be an active player or not. Remember, it is not gauged by big grandiose ideas or actions, because the smallest of actions can be the seed of what changes the world.

What I want to add to your resume is powerful, spiritual knowledge. It will arm you with bullet proof wisdom ready to be used to inspire and excel you through this final adventure. All I ask is just give me a read and you'll see how true it is. After that, I pray you will use this knowledge to help bring this world back to its senses.

CHAPTER RECAP

- We are all internally connected to the truth.

- Living a fulfilling life takes wisdom.

- We are an essential part of the collective whole of humanity.

- We are all here for a reason/ every person counts.

- God created Elders for a reason.

- Sharing is a fundamental gift from God as well as inspiration.

CHAPTER 2

Teaching an Old Dog New Tricks

Teaching an old dog new tricks has been a common scenario in my life. I have had so many different careers, and each new career had its built-in excitement as well as its many challenges. I had to perform, I had to learn, and I had to make it happen. Unlike many who found early on what their life's work was, for me, that wasn't the case…for better or for worse.

But the obvious point I'm saying is: learning new skills may, in fact, come easier than you think. Looking back, I am sure most of us would agree we had to do it so many times in our lives out of necessity that it became familiar territory.

Life events that alter the status quo have been our

biggest motivators. And by now, we have faced most of them. A financial crisis, a death in the family, death of a spouse, a returning son or daughter, grandchildren, great-grandchildren, illness, a partner issue. The list can be endless. This is life, and we, by the nature of who we are, should know it best.

Now let's be a little more upbeat! After all we are talking about new "tricks".

I am sure each of my examples must have conjured up some emotions—some good, some not so good. But we also know by now that emotions can be fickle and can change from good to bad and bad to good.

The reason I chose to discuss this is that deciding to go down a new road of life will bring up emotions. Some are feelings of doubt, fear, excitement etc., and all those emotions, specifically the negative ones. It must be looked at carefully. But consider your most proven resource which is your experience and proven instincts. We all know there are few if any absolutes in life. And on the other hand, let's take a good look at the potential benefits verses the potential downside.

I know this may sound silly, but sometimes we tend to forget how skilled we are in life, and how much we take it for granted.

I remember when my son attended a new school in northern California and I became a very involved parent, joining weekly meetings with the other parents. Of course, I was the oldest parent by decades. Not to pay homage to myself or brag, but honestly, I soon became aware of how much I knew that seemed common knowledge to me but really wasn't. Surprisingly, those younger parents were wide-eyed with my suggestions and knowledge, and truly appreciative. To the credit of the new principal, she scheduled an hour of time each week to meet with me privately and talk about suggestions I made. Not bad. Also, the fact that my son was a model "A" student and a great athlete (and an amazing kid in general) seemed to also point out that not all my ideas were just theory, but I had a walking-talking-shining example.

Had I ever done anything like this before? No, not at all. The element that motivated me into this new arena was obviously my son. But aside from that the real lesson here is that my instincts said I can do this, even though in the eyes of more traditional academics, I was far from qualified. Who at our age thinks about education besides, of course, those who have come from that field? And in fact, that experience launched me into a new career later as working as a substitute teacher, and tutor which I continue today, which by the way, I love.

At our age, we have opinions—and talent—and many abilities. Should all of these built-up human resources go to waste? Hell no! So, what is stopping us? Nothing for some of us, but for those who have the "wear with all" but are *stuck,* let's look at that.

What stopped me in the past were my insecurities. They were nasty and downright evil. They were brilliant in their arguments. But the good news is, they can be defeated. Yes, it can be difficult but, in fact, we are capable of making most, if not all, disappear.

When I got involved in my son's education it was somewhat uncomfortable, but it wasn't terrible. I felt I was capable. Yes, I would tread carefully…one step at a time, so to speak. And this method I would pass on to you as well. But the most important thing was that I stepped into this new world armed with 69 years of living experience that proved to be an amazing and surprisingly powerful asset.

Now, for me my motivation was my kid's education, but for you the choices are actually limitless. A friend of mine is a member of the community art committee. Another is a member of a smart growth group. The list goes on and is truly endless. But it's most important to find a *passion* and let its power quiet any of those negative voices.

But to add to your pocket of "personal tools", I have unveiled a few secrets that I continue to use to this day. In teaching you these new "spiritual tools," (a better word than trick), it will diminish many of your doubts and will encourage you to move beyond your fears. It will absolutely eradicate the negative, limited thinking that tries so hard to keep you from finding something that makes you happy.

These tools are not new but in fact have been utilized in the spiritual community for thousands of years, with impeccable success. The first one I want to talk about is called, "restriction".

RESTRICTION

Means simply: do not react. Hold off emotionally and mentally. DO NOT PUT A LABEL to anything. The simple reason is that your label may very well BE WRONG!

Remember, all that I reveal is coming from the spiritual community where the belief is that we are not God, but we have the DNA of God. That means we have God-like qualities to do things the right way and what defines the right way, is "happiness", free from pain and suffering. Learning "restriction" will be a big step in getting you there. But it is a learning process.

Of course, we will be challenged because that's part of

the system. But that's what spirituality is all about, though we will discuss that in my "Spirituality" chapter later on. For now, let's stay on course, which is "teaching an old dog new tricks" and our first tool called, "restriction".

Restriction is a tool for everything in life. For the purpose of venturing into unfamiliar territory, we will just use examples where restriction will serve you well. Sounds kind of odd that something one would restrict will move one forward but let me explain....

The best example I can come up with is to look at our past. We all have memories where we said something we regret to this day and opportunities we passed over even though every bone in our body told us to go for it and didn't. In most cases we reacted in a compulsive way. We opted to listen to those negative voices in our heads, mostly of doubt and we lost out on a wonderful opportunity. If we practiced "restriction" and refused to allow those voices to interfere, life could have changed for the better. The trick, of course, is to take the time to check out your voices and see if they are holding you back or moving you forward. Trust your instincts!

That's the first tool. Practice it. Practice it in small situations until you get the feel of it and then expand it as you get more comfortable. Restricting those negative thoughts is powerful and can change your life big-time.

I mentioned this is a two-step process. The second step is called "conscious pro activity". Yes, it's a mouthful. Simply put, it is to be consciously aware of being proactive for the right reasons. And when I say for the right reasons I mean reasons that are spiritual in nature. When I volunteered my time with my son's school it was an honest attempt to help and contribute to others. That's spiritual. It was not an ego trip for me but an opportunity to use my abilities, insights, experience, etc. to share and help. It was pure, and thus it worked. It became a "spiritual opportunity" in helping others.

Sharing is the name of the game. If you go out again into the world with the desire of sharing what you have learned, you become a powerful entity. The right people will acknowledge it. If you are sincere and your ego is put aside, going out again in the world, and entering a new venture, will have a different sense of purpose. In short, they will see that you are there to give, not to take.

This second tool, if looked at closely, will change your world around you. It has the capability to remove virtually 99% of your emotional doubt and insecurities. I know that's a big statement.

If my words are going to have any impact at all, we must all agree that there is a reason for all of us to be here on earth at this time. Without that assumption, my words will have little or no impact. So, you might say this is where the tire meets the road, and those of you who are not convinced with that concept, bite your tongue and stay with me anyway. Hold off your judgments and you may discover this amazing new approach to life that will turn you into an instant powerhouse of positivity. It will also help define your next step and keep you on the proper path. Doing things for the right reasons changes the playing field tremendously.

If anything, life has taught me to love what you do. Yes, years ago I might have taken jobs I wasn't thrilled about, but now there should be no excuses for that. Find that place in your heart where in the workplace where you can be happy. It will propel you beyond your expectations when your heart is truly the driving force. You will also learn the power of the heart and how many are misconceived thinking how weak and vulnerable the heart is. To the contrary, the heart should be the engine of choice that will drive you to where true happiness resides.

CHAPTER RECAP

- Learning new skills can come easy.

- Remember how skilled we already are.

- Find your passion and use it as a driving force.

- Restriction as a tool.

- Be consciously proactive.

- Share.

- Do things for the right reasons.

CHAPTER 3

Your Mind is a Beautiful Thing

The mind is a beautiful thing and a precious gift indeed. But I have also found that the mind can be either your best friend or your worst enemy. So how does that work? Does the mind have a mind of its own? Mind you, (no pun intended) ☺ I am not a Dr. Horowitz. Instead, I am someone who has chosen the spiritual versus the clinical path and has found very interesting simple answers that are easy to apply with a solid awareness of making sense. Are you still with me?

After all, doesn't it all start with the mind? I think of it as the control center that is never off duty. Even when we're asleep, it's still hard at work. So how can we harness this amazing feature of the human being? Without going to the scientific community, let's take a more practical approach. Let's look at the mind's main product: *thought*.

In the spiritual world, I have found that thoughts are an expression, and the two thoughts that are most expressed are either: positive thought which is the "soul consciousness"; and secondly: the negative thought or thoughts that come from the "darker side". It's that simple.

In the world of spirituality, those two opposite thoughts are equally available to us. And that is one of God's greatest gifts, which is "free will". If I may…let's tie those two ideas together with a little anecdote about my two kids when they were still in the single digits.

When my son and daughter were very young, I told them that they have two angels: the negative angel perched on one shoulder and the positive angel sitting on the other. The negative angel only knows to be bad, whispering only negative things into their ear. His words are "mean": words of jealousy, yelling words, angry words, etc., "It's his fault!" "No, it's her fault!" Got it? And the positive angel who knows and says only positive things, such as: "Thank you", "I'm sorry", "I love you" etc. And most important, the positive side encourages us not to say all those harsh words and actions. These voices, according to most spiritual teachings, are actually real. So, I would say to the both of my children, "hey, you guys, be careful which angel you listen to."

Whether true or not, I thought how profound that concept is. How empowering it is that now, at such young ages, they actually have a choice of who influences their thought: good angel or bad angel. And now that my kids have a choice—good or bad angel—it becomes their own free choices to make. How easy can it get?

Well, of course it's never that easy, but it did make their

decisions visible and easily blamable to an outside force: good angel, good choice/bad angel, bad choice.

So now their own mind is at work. Now they themselves can take hold of their free choice of which one they listen to, and easily experience the results themselves. Of course, along with that I would say, "You do good things, good things happen. Do bad things and bad things happen."

Not to say my kids are perfect-perfect but it does give them a method of how to make choices, a sense of right and wrong, an awareness of choices and consequences, and most important, how that system actually works.

This little and simple lesson greatly helped my kids recognize those voices and mentally deal with them as forces trying to influence them. Because these forces came from the outside, it is their choice, their "free will" to accept it and take it in or reject it. Got it?

The real beauty to the system is that every time they reject the negative voices, or angels as we called them, it made them feel good. It made them feel they had made the right choice on their own! And in the world of spirituality, this is how one elevates to another higher spiritual notch. It is God's reward.

Now let's bring this to our world, to you and me.

Let's say you refrain from saying a not so nice thing to your wife, husband, or friend. The mere fact that you refrained from listening to your own bad angel, you were given points. I call them, "God Points". In the world of spirituality, and in your world on earth, these points are very, very important. The point being…by being aware of these voices and recognizing whether they are positive voices or negative voices goes a very long way in taking control of your mind and the actions you take. Simple rule for all to follow: Do negative get negative; do positive, get positive. The only caveat is that sometimes the results are not necessarily so instant...so be patient. I promise the payoff will come. And by the way, my kids still use this system today.

THE IDEA

The next topic of the mind I want to talk about is "The Idea".

As we all know by now there are good ideas and bad ideas, just like the good angel and the bad angel. I am sure we have all have experienced both. The interesting thing is that the mind will accept either one without discrimination unless something else intervenes. The mind will accept the Republican Party, Democratic Party, socialism, democracy, terrorism—you name it. It appears as if it doesn't seem to matter. And yet people will dedicate their lives for some ideas and even die for these ideas... the mind will house them all. And Lord knows I've had my share of good ideas, and my share of very, very bad ideas. So how can we maintain that positive path and stay with, and recognize, the good ideas??

When people compare the mind to a computer where information is stored, their analogy seems reasonable, logical, and even scientific. But that's where we run into a "dead end". I may be wrong, but I believe this is also where science comes to a dead end as well.

But as the saying goes, "When one door closes another door opens." This is the exact door I want to open...so step right in! This door, I believe opens to a road...a road of *free choice*.

Because our mind is continually being bombarded with

thousands and thousands of external influences, some good, some not, it makes it more and more difficult to feel that we are free—really free—to make clear, uninfluenced decisions. What the heck to do?

Well, you may not like the answer, and then again, the fact is…no one is perfect. Life is a learning journey, and making mistakes is an important part of the process. How many failures did Edison have before he invented the light bulb?

I know someone out there is taking a big sigh of relief. Good for you!

To begin, we need to be aware of the place inside ourselves where our decisions are made.

When making decisions, take notice whether it is being influenced by negative factors like anger or jealousy, or other negative emotions. As a senior, I ask you, when have those negative-influenced decisions ever turned out well?

For me, they never have. So, I just don't make decisions when mad, or when I am under the influence of other negative emotions. I take a breather and simply, resist uttering out things you know you are going to regret later.

Another method I use for making better choices is to determine if my actions are meant to just benefit my ego. Examples are easy to find, and become very visible when the excitement, the luster, the gratifications shortly sink and the thrill disappears.

On the other side of the coin, how fulfilling is it when I use my heart as a gauge. It is like the time I helped my son with some problem or when I gave my daughter a letter of appreciation or bought her an appropriate birthday gift.

Other personal examples of things I have done which

had lasting good feelings are donating to a worthy charity or cause, giving flowers, a smile, giving of myself, sharing, avoid arguments and negative comments.

Later, I have a chapter that is titled, "Your Ego" which will get into many of those actions in more detail, but for now, open to and acknowledge those thoughts of being unselfish, thinking of others, being kind, being thoughtful, etc. You get the point.

After all, most of these small decisions make up a good part of our waking hours. I have found that if I keep my good angel happy as much as possible I wind up having a pretty good day. You see, good angel decisions seem to take into account all of me, as if my whole body responds to that decision in a positive way, contrary to the other kinds of decisions that may only find partial and fleeting pleasure.

Think about it, making the good angel happy may sound somewhat childish, but who cares? We're seniors. We have a right to our childish side, especially if it makes us happy as well.

Here's a word of caution: the negative angels never give up. They forever try to influence you, so we need to be always on our toes. The good news is that the more we do this, the easier we recognize its voice, thus making it easier to reject.

Take worrying for example. When, in your long history of worrying, has it ever paid off? For me it was "never". It comes from the dark side because worrying is not proactive. It does nothing but create anxiety. The answer: don't let it in.

Your mind is like any other muscle that will get stronger and stronger as you use it. So, the message is to use it properly. Like the saying goes: "Garbage in garbage out" or, positive in positive out. Just be more mindful of what you accept in your mind. I promise the more positive ideas or thoughts you put into your mind the more positive life becomes.

Be a spiritual mind bodybuilder like my kids—it works no matter what age. The more positive thoughts you allow inside you leaves less room for the negative. The voice that comes from the good angel is a tool that can lead you to where the pot of gold resides.

Remember, in life there are no free rides, so it's best to have acquired as many of these spiritual tools to really reap its benefits. The more spiritual knowledge we fill our mind with, the less stress you have. Some call these tools "Universal Knowledge". This is what this book is all about: raising your awareness, or consciousness, as to how things really work with the mind. This knowledge promises to free us from anxiety, fear, chaos, emotional suffering, and all sorts of other bad things that originate from the mind. Even science finally backs me on that. So, for me to stay healthy and keep your mind healthy, I go to the classic spiritual teachings of wisdom, which also serves as my medicine for the mind.

FREE WILL

Think about it. We have started life with the mind in its pure state—open and free of any influences, giving us this amazing gift from God called, *free will*. Again, according to many spiritual teachings, free will is one of the most important gifts from God. I like this concept because it takes us out of what they call, *victim consciousness*. This means that ultimately, *we* are responsible for what we accept into our mind. It's our free will—free choice, right? So, without going too deep, be aware of those lurking Madison Avenue executives—the bad angels—trying to steal our free will. It is God's treasured gift so, the bottom line of all this is…be careful who you listen to, and who or what you allow into your mind.

I know you're all grown up but what I'm saying has no age.

I continually check myself against *agenda spins*, which are everywhere. If I stay balanced in my mind and allow myself to look deeper, and on occasion, pause, I can see the root of things and allow the truth to emerge.

Stay true to your instincts and listen to your angels— the good angels. Close the door to those nasty, bad, or negative angels, shutting them out and only letting the good pour in! Being *balanced* inside is the real key.

MIND OVER MATTER

This last part of the mind chapter I want to talk about it may not suit everyone, but I feel compelled to mention it, especially to those who have already been on the spiritual path. That is the mystical side of spirituality—the place where miracles occur, also known as, *mind over matter*.

What is even more amazing is that this gift is handed over to us as living proof of our DNA that connects us to God himself, allowing us to witness those miracles first hand.

Once again, I have a separate chapter on *miracles* but the point I wanted to express is that our mind has trillions of neurons creating energy forces no one has come close to understanding. Even science admits we have barely reached the capacity of our brain—our mind.

Remember, this is God's work and He made it that way for a reason.

It's my belief we are certain to reach that point when we will truly see and know God. I believe he wants us to figure it out, and only when we're ready and we've earned it. We even have a name for it, *elevated consciousness*.

He gave us the hardware, and now with elevated consciousness as our software, it will reveal itself as it already has to certain elevated souls throughout history.

It is predicted that there will be a tipping point, when enough people get to this spiritual consciousness, the world will revert to the "Garden of Eden" once again and forever. It will be at the end of the rainbow so to speak.

But this prize of prizes does not come easy. So, as a hint to the end game, and to keep us on track, I believe that God gave us the ability to create miracles to encourage us to go deeper, like a spiritual carrot. If we really look closer and notice these miracles, we see they are everywhere. Humanity is just used to those grandiose miracles that make it easy for everyone to see.

History is filled with stories of miracle after miracle to where even science can't discount them. And yet, they keep on trying to disprove them again and again. So, in an odd way, it's like an unwelcomed relative who keeps on knocking at the door and won't go away. Except this time, it is not a relative but God himself at the door saying, "Hi, it's me again. Can I come in?"

Eventually, I predict it will be science that ultimately figures it out. Yes, they will be the last to fall but when they do it they will fall hard...and the final miracle will appear. There are hints of that happening already.

THE OTHER SIDE TO THE DARKNESS IS THE LIGHT

I would like to throw you a curve ball! Let's say this bad angel isn't so bad after all. What if that bad angel is in fact our greatest ally? That is exactly what many spiritual teachings say. Confused?

I'm bringing this amazing concept to our awareness as another example of what our mind is capable of. Just to simply understand this thought alone can change our entire lives from a big negative to a very big positive.

It's actually very simple. Think about your own life. What made you rise to heights you never imagined? The answer I think we all can agree on would be the demanding situations, impossible situations, and/or situations we had to work hard to overcome. Well, here lies the answer, *forging forward and never allowing these challenges to get the best of us.*

There is another part of us that will intuitively want to fight those negative impulses (negative angels) that tell us to quit. However, we want to fight with our mind and reject their influences until we finally get to our goal. Whether we understand the process or not this is the process God gave us and is again housed in our mind.

Simply put, when the negative forces come into our lives and we *reject* them, the positive door opens. It's the law. When we don't buy into negative people and even demanding situations, the negative energy weakens and our positive power increases.

Thus, here lies another universal law, *The Law of Cause and Effect.* Don't feed the fire and soon the fire will die. And when it dies, the smoke clears and blue skies with smiles appear, and another gold star gets pinned on your chest by the Big Guy himself. Remember, this *is* His system and it all begins and ends in your mind.

What good is it to believe in God and then believe that God shouldn't be a part of your decision-making? That would be ludicrous. God loves you... I mean *really* loves you. He loves you beyond your comprehension. If your mind really gets that concept the mind becomes a powerful driver in your life in a very positive way.

And so, that is why he invented, *tough love*. He knows when things are appreciated or even cherished. It's when we work for them. And God, in his infinite wisdom, gave us part of Him to make sure we had no excuses. He gave us our brain, our mind that has endless potential and the awesome ability to move through life and beyond. But remember it all came from Him, not you. And if we acknowledge that in our mind, and continue our path, one day, we will figure it all out. I mean ALL the secrets, and I mean ALL of them. Amazing! That our potential is ready to be released through this miracle of our brain and its infinite expression called the mind.

CHAPTER RECAP

- There are positive thoughts and negative thoughts.

- Good Angel/soul thinking.

- Bad Angel never gives up.

- Free will.

- The positive side of the negative.

CHAPTER 4

Your Ego.
Can we talk about it?

If you are going to get anything out of this book, you had better man-up (you too ladies) to take a good hard look at our biggest enemy, our biggest obstacle, our biggest nemesis...our EGO!

The problem with the *ego* is that no matter how hard you try, you'll never get rid of it. That's the bad news. The good news is, no one ever has. So, what's the point, you ask? Well, let me put it this way. It's like in spirituality, the main idea is to become *God like*. We all know becoming God is impossible but striving to be *God like* isn't. In fact, just going for an unattainable goal is actually very common, especially among high achievers. The same applies with taking on the goal of eliminating the ego.

The nice thing about taking on the ego, it offers the biggest rewards in becoming a happy and fulfilled person. But the first thing is to learn to recognize what the ego even looks like. Once you begin to learn to identify your ego, you have completed the most crucial step of all. The ensuing step will be the next important action, and it is, *what to do next.*

Here's an easy example with a multiple-choice A, B, or C answers. Ready? Think of yourself having an amazing meal with your significant other at your favorite restaurant. Everything seems perfect. As the meal is coming to an end you think to yourself, with a smile, this couldn't have been any better. Out from nowhere, someone walks by, bumps your waiter, and that hundred-dollar bottle of red wine in his hand drops on your lap and spills all over you! Boom! Omg!

You jump out of your seat, mouth wide open and then… Be honest.

1.   You get up, mad as hell, call the waiter a clumsy fool and demand some kind of restitution?

2.   You get up, restrain yourself a little but demand to see the manager, saying in your mind, I should at least say something and not look like a fool.

3.   This third option would be completely different. Though you might get up it wouldn't be about your own personal concerns but to make sure no one, aside from yourself got hurt or got affected. Tell the waiter don't worry and it wasn't his fault and give him a nice reassuring smile.

I love this challenge because if you look at the different choices of action you can take, it can clearly expose the size of your ego. But what's the point here? and make it *red faced,* and that's a good thing.

From the spiritual perspective, let's say you are standing on top of this beautiful mountain with this unbelievable view of the ocean. It is the perfect day…perfect clouds, perfect amount of birds flying in the air, perfect temperature, and the perfect breeze. Life is good! You close your eyes; you savor the moment.

Then slowly, you open your eyes for another joyful moment. Without warning, appearing from nowhere, is this thick, dense fog. Oh, no! No view, no warm breeze, no birds, no beautiful sky…just this ugly gray cloud that overshadows everything—thick and blinding. Well, you have experienced your ego. That dense fog is what your ego does. It is the negative voice to everything—relationships, love, happiness—everything that is good, everything that is beautiful.

The interesting thing is that all those good and beautiful things are still there; they are just hidden by this greatest of all negative energy known to man as the ego.

Amazing. It acts like the most dangerous and sneaky of predators. It is also the greediest and determined of predators—ever persistent. Learn to know its power…how demanding it is and how it will attack anything good at all costs. It's an amazing adversary. It's sneaky, creepy, and expresses itself through many, many ways.

The ego in one form or another is why we're here on earth. According to some of the spiritual community, of which I will speak about in a future chapter, the ego is also a creation from God. Yes, that's true. How could something so evil, so destructive, come from God?

Let's look at it this way… Let's say God is our boss at work. He's fair, honest, and cares for his workers but is tough…very tough. He is the type that pushes us very hard. But he knows how to get us out of our comfort zones and help to take us to the next level of capabilities.

Let's say one day he came up with the ultimate challenge: if you can cross this finish line, you not only get the blue ribbon but the brass ring of life…pure and true freedom. So, he now calls his invention, his final new challenge at work, the ego. He says, "Here is the challenge…destroy this and you've won!"

Think about it. What a concept. Yes, I say it is! But this time the rewards reach out to the universe. If you think I am overstating it, try it… Prove me wrong. No, prove me right!

I heard from a friend the other day. He was frustrated about some financial institution that was giving him a tough time. It frustrated him to the point where he couldn't sleep, and his mind was flooded with thoughts of launching multiple lawsuits…or multiple bullets.

I wrote back saying that when I experience those combative situations and feel my blood pressure rising, I realize my ego has made its presence and is trying to take over. However, once I acknowledge the existence of my ego in the equation the anger begins to dissolve. I can see the situation more clearly and soon a solution comes to mind. So, it's possible. I can't tell you how true this is because its vulnerability is equally amazing—once it's exposed, once we can see it, guess what? It shrinks like a busted thief in the night.

But facing one's ego can almost be like facing a burning fire. One gets panicky, scared, and overwhelmed. However, remember, ego is also a creation of God. So, we should assume God knew what he was doing when he gave us such an adversary. But the crucial point one needs to keep in mind is that God wants us to win. But like courting a woman, it takes work. And if you are successful, the rewards are bountiful. You just need to acquire some tools, and hopefully the ones I'll provide will take the scares away. You may not win every battle, but the fact that you chose to take on the ego makes you an instant winner. And remember, its God who set up this encounter but also keep in mind he is also your partner. Now, let's look at the enemy's weak points.

Like I said. On the bright side…you have taken the first step: that is…you and I (and God looking over our shoulders) are ready to uncover its ugly face.

The ego, like any stealth enemy is a master of disguise. It can hide behind a smile, a tone in our voice, a facial expression, and especially a thought, to name a few. We must be on our guard. This is part of the game of life where the stakes are high, but so are the rewards. If we want to improve our relationships with friends and love ones, we need to take on a warrior pose, as if we were in the middle of hostile territory. So, what are we looking for, and what does this enemy look like?

Ego expresses itself through anger, jealousy, pride, shyness, judgments, and feelings of being smarter, taller, or better, the importance of winning an argument. The list goes on and on and exposing one's ego requires vigilance. The more you become aware of your ego, the more will surface. It is part of the healing process so don't freak out. It's as if you're in the middle of the emotional jungle, ever alert, keeping aware of whether any of those feelings surface. Don't kid yourself; these ego traits are as lethal as any monster out there. You are taking on humanity's most fierce and feared opponent, and like I said before, the rewards are everlasting and far surpass anything you have done before. Now the obvious question is, how the heck do I do this?

Like any warrior taking on the enemy, you'll need weapons along with acquired skills. You don't have to be big and strong. What you do need is desire as the driving force and, along with my words of guidance, you'll so soon be on your way to face the enemy. Surprisingly, one of the most important weapons we have is "taking the moment". We spoke of this before. We called it restriction. The ego likes to be expressed almost always in a reactive way…like a striking venomous snake. But instead of venom, it lashes out and takes the form of myriad negative emotions. So, think before you open your mouth.

My son likes to play chess online. What these games allow you to do is take back moves as far as you want and re-strategize. Obviously, he never loses, but also, he gets to see his mistakes. The restriction rule also applies here. The one thing that is profoundly different, however, is it's impossible to take back our moves, our angry outcries, our stupid jealous comments. But what if we could have taken that "pause" before those words left our mouth? What if those words were never spoken? In some cases, a single word or misplaced comment may have changed our destiny. But let's not cry over spilled milk. Of course, we have all done it. And sure, we have all screwed up.

This is where it's completely okay to be the Monday morning quarterback for oneself because we are never short on opportunities to do better the next time. But don't fool yourself…the ego is there ever ready to ooze through the cracks in our defense. It won't disappear; it never does.

The difference is that we are now going to show a few of its colors. It is now up to us to keep the guards on duty. The only real homework I'm assigning is to write down your own ego issues. If you're brave enough, you could ask a good friend or spouse to add a few. Believe me, there is never a shortage. It may seem like an agonizing and humbling exercise. It is, and it is supposed to be. But the benefits will be beyond your imagination. To help in your effort I will offer some suggestions that have, and continue to, help me keep my feet on the ground, and my ego somewhat in view.

The number one suggestion is never hesitate to say you're sorry, mostly on those occasions when you are innocent of charges. The concept of being "right" or "wrong" usually comes into play here, and may I say, LET IT GO! Think of all those situations and arguments defending silly right and wrong arguments that only led to resentment and bad feelings. To further the point, how many of those encounters do you remember what the facts were really about? So, in short...remember it was all about your ego, pure and simple.

On that subject, if you are wrong about something, no matter how small an issue, *admit it*, ADMIT BEING WRONG. It's sexy, whether it comes out of a woman's or a guy's mouth. But mostly, it's freeing.

Secondly: don't take things for granted. Wake up and thank God for another opportunity to enjoy the day. I promise, there are many who won't get the privilege.

Thirdly: appreciate not only the day you were given but appreciate as many things you can count. One day, when my son Anton was eleven or twelve, he came up with over 100.

Fourth: Forgive. Remember, to forgive is really for your benefit. It is a matter of healing...letting go. You will not change that other person but what you'll do is release the anger that has been occupying space in your heart too long.

Fifth: be thankful. Thank people a lot. It's very good to diminish the ego while making others feel good. Every time you thank someone it injects positive energy directly to their heart, their soul. And your own.

The sixth is to just be on your guard. Again, if you screw up—and you will—don't worry, another opportunity to do better is usually only moments away.

The ego has been honored with many books written about it. It has created kingdoms, dynasties, armies, navies, and remarkable stories in both fiction and nonfiction. But if you peel away the glitter, the ego is the single most destructive force on the planet, responsible for the killings of women and defenseless children, broken families and friendships in countless ways, wars that last forever, the list is endless.

It can, however, be significantly beaten but it does take work. The effort can lead you into the most rewarding benefit life has to offer. You'll soon discover how you have been held captive by all those feelings of anger, being the victim, pride, jealousy, etc. Soon a clearer view comes into play. To be no longer angry—no longer the victim—will lead to a sense of tranquil peace that takes over the space and the people around you. This is real power. It is power that will heal, create love, and other positive actions that will provide benefits far more valuable than all the gold on the planet, or even that new car you may be driving, or that new expensive suit you're wearing.

CHAPTER RECAP

- The ego is a stealth predator.
- The ego is why we are here on earth.
- Learn to recognize the ego.
- Pause.
- Tools of combating the ego are:

  a. Saying, "Sorry"

  b. There are no rights or wrongs

  c. Be appreciative

  d. Anger, jealousy, resentment, are all ego traits.

CHAPTER 5

Thank God for
THE BIG PICTURE

How often does something take over our mind and it won't go away? It could be as small as a comment someone made, a bump a person gives you in a restaurant, or even a look—and, oh, can those looks get you going.

It's amazing how these small, or even big, issues can take us off track. Why am I so taken in? Why am I so susceptible to that emotional sucker punch that pushed that button? Well, we did all read the chapter on *Ego,* so this chapter will definitely help you keep your ego in check.

Coming center stage, I want to introduce… "THE BIG PICTURE!" It's modest in nature, but don't fool yourself it is very, very powerful. It is a great tool I try and remember as much as possible, and it gives unselfishly. Even the thought of it relaxes me because it never fails.

I can't remember how many times I have gotten sucked into the small stuff, or even the big stuff, and my entire day turned to crap! I'm entrapped within those invisible emotional prison bars with no way out, doomed to everlasting depression.

Wait! Is it possible... Do we have the "Spiritual Calvary" in this movie? Yes, I think we do. And it's called "The Big Picture".

With its arrival, looking at the big picture of things puts me in a space that relieves the pressure. It creates a peace of mind allowing my better, clearer vision of positive energy to intercede. It neutralizes the emotional blues, and yes, it even brings me to another insight that makes things so much better.

The Big Picture is in the movie of my life I can never live without. It is the guru, the wise and gentle one. It is the voice that says, "Sandy, take hold of yourself. Let's take another look, but this time, relax and open up, and let's look at what is really at play here. Yes, open up and remove the narrow blinders, and look at the big picture. It will dissolve the anxiety, the anger, the frustration, and replace it with *amazing insights and produce worthy wisdom.* It is truly remarkable.

Every time I get caught up in a situation, I remind myself to stop and look at the big picture, another reality unfolds before my very eyes—a reality that removes the veil, so I can see clarity in the situation. It's like enjoying the benefits of being the Monday night quarterback on any day of the week. I become very committed to this tool because seeing the big picture is, of course, right. It's always right.

Last night, my son pissed me off. What crime did he commit? He pushed that button called "disrespect". Thank God, I resisted being reactive and looked at the big picture. I took the moment and reminded myself that my son is a teenager, and that, itself is challenging. Once I connected to the big picture, I also realized my inflamed ego wrapped around my hurt feelings. So, I regrouped and communicated with my son from a much more rational and proactive position. In the end, he said he was sorry and I got a better picture of his internal identity struggle. We both benefited and avoided an ugly scene. I took a deep breath of relief. So, thank you once again "the big picture".

To see the big picture, you have to do the same thing as on Google maps and hit the minus sign to get a broader view. Once you look at the issue from afar, it doesn't seem so foggy. And the more you hit that minus sign, the less it can even be seen.

Not only does this method provide a better perspective of things and give you breathing room, but it helps elevate your perspective, both emotionally and spiritually, just like it did between Anton and me.

Think about it. The big picture opens the door to a fresher view, and if you are really on top of it you can see where you messed up. Being so deeply tied to the issue or problem just puts on blinders.

As I've said many times so far, try to recognize the ego in the middle of your anxiety. I promise you'll find it accounts for 100% of the issue. The big picture will help you see it and greatly help in unveiling the wolf hiding in sheep clothes. The wonderful thing about this technique is that you can use it even after the fact. Discovering these new insights is exhilarating and very, very exciting.

I would like you to pay attention to something that can

be another great tool: your instincts. I honestly can't tell you where that special feeling comes from but when I pay attention to my instincts it helps me remember to connect to the big picture. Personally, it seems to be connected to my soul trying to voice out, "Hey you! Remember the big picture"! It's like someone threw me a life buoy in a sea of emotional darkness. What a life-saver.

Life's most fulfilling treasures are not always a pot of gold. In fact, the lasting treasures are those things that feed the soul, like the magic of using this technique of the big picture.

CHAPTER RECAP

- The power of seeing the Big Picture.

- Open up and remove those narrow blinders.

- It will produce amazing insights and worthy wisdom.

- Use it as the Monday Night Quarterback.

- Use it with your instincts.

Skye

CHAPTER 6

"Get Out!
All you naysayers!"

"**G**et out of my way, one way or another!"
No, I'm not driving my super charged Porsche down Hollywood Boulevard but rather, getting those naysayers out of my life.

YOU ARE NEEDED! Do you think that you were created for no reason? Do you think you are still alive just to take up space? Think of what you accomplished already in your life. What talents have you uncovered during your lifework? In sales, marketing, medicine, law, education, parenting, etc. So, what tells you to stop? What voice tells you it's time to do *nothing*!

If you believe in your common sense doing *nothing,* it just makes no sense at all.

At our age, doing nothing should be the last thing that comes into our mind. It's like collecting gold year after year and then dying without spending any of it. What a waste! Whether it could have been used for a well-earned vacation or given to a worthy cause, not using that resource is a crime. The same goes for your resource of experience and knowledge.

So, the next question that might pop into your brain is, where do I start? Well, first look to see if you have a secret wish list…a secret to-do list—or a bucket list, as it's called now. I can't tell you how important this is. Even if you can't think of something now, just start thinking.

The mistake I made was that I kept on thinking of the same recurring list…over and over again. It was a lengthy list because I have had an extensive list of careers. I actually thought of being a writer, but I thought it was too lofty of a goal left only to those who wear sport jackets with leather elbow patches (pipes are out these days). And here I am writing away in coffee houses and beyond.

It was only after a series of events that the light bulb went on.

For those who know a little about me, I have a teenage son and a preteen daughter. Consequently, when Anton is doing a sport or when I'm participating in some way at his school, I am the elder amongst the forty/thirty-year-old parents.

In California, I became so involved in Anton's school that I attended their weekly meetings with the other parents and their awe-inspiring principal. For me, these meetings became very empowering. I heard their well-meaning comments, complaints, concerns and questions. A very good friend of mine, a sort of mentor, once told me, "Sandy, I never want to go to a meeting and be the smartest person at the table." It was great advice for sure. But when surrounded by forty thirty-somethings I have found I'd better be the smartest person at the table!

The ego—hopefully the "healthy" ego—imploded, and somehow fired up every neuron in my brain, and I was smart again...at least to them. But in fact, it wasn't my intelligence that came up with the answers. It was my *experience* in life. Things, ideas, I just took for granted that everyone knew, but to my surprise, didn't. Boy, was that an eye opener.

I know I am preaching to the choir, but these well-minded, hardworking, bright, caring, loving parents were nothing less than advanced kids hiding in forty-something skin. I know you know what I'm talking about. So, I said to myself, "Hey, I recognized these kids who are just experiencing receding hairlines. They're a piece a cake!"

Suddenly, my confidence reached heights of unexplored territory. Oh, the joy I felt. If anyone wants to experience "the young pill" that was it. And guess what, if you were there with me in that room, I'll bet you'd be sitting up straighter, voice a little deeper, and feeling a whole lot better about yourself.

These are people who opened their minds and listened to my voice. They connected to my senior ship of experience and the words I spoke and the guidance I gave and voiced their appreciation.

Stupidly, our culture has decided to go it alone without the guidance of "elders", and stupidly, we are buying into it. Excuse me, I did not come up with the idea of having well-seasoned, well-experienced, intelligent people who have gone through life, so it can be passed on. What if the people of Israel decided Moses was too old and only relied on twenty-, thirty-, or even forty-year old's to lead them to the Promised Land. Oh my!

Or let's say, George Washington, Winston Churchill, or those of the Chinese culture, or the American Indian removed their system of leadership through the guidance headed by elders. Okay, I'm not saying we "elder cockers" have not screwed up, but aren't our mistakes really our pot of gold?

My theory to that can best be explained by those people who haven't had the blessings of abundant challenges in their lives. They have experienced few obstacles; few ups and not many downs. Have you been to a party where there were people who had it that easy in life? If so, try having a meaningful conversation with them and you'll end up crying from boredom.

So, let me go back to the point at hand.

Don't listen to the naysayers. In fact, the naysayers may be your only obstacle. Imagine if you eliminated their voice from your life, or your own head, what the new road would look like.

I realize much of what I have to say is repetitive, but I feel compelled to keep reminding you, so you may see for yourself how much negative input we seniors have been getting. Yes, it is a battle, but honestly it boils down to whether you want to find true happiness.

I only say that because I can say with absolute certainty that I have found true happiness, and believe it or not, the golden key was in my head and my heart all the time. One of the most important steps I needed to take was to clear my mind of negativity and negative people. It only serves someone else's agenda, never mine.

I guess the point I'm making is, don't listen to other people's made-up assumptions, especially about you and your worth. We all know the saying about assumptions, right?

We assume too much even when life has taught us not to…yet we are perfectly fine allowing others to assume we are not needed. OMG (you all know what OMG means, right?) Please, don't buy into that. Only God has that right.

If I would ask what the condition of the world is today, what would you say? It's a big question, right? Well, if it was me, I would not typically ask a local politician, or a thirty- or forty-year-old someone, or especially a twenty-year-old someone. Get the point?

We are needed more than ever before because the younger generation actually thinks they can do it alone. They are like inexperienced hunters going into the deepest bowels of the forest looking to take down a grizzly bear. Any idiot knows their chance of making it out alive is about zero! Excuse me for getting a little feisty ☺. The point being: The Creator gave us lineage for a reason. He gave us wisdom (King Solomon) for a reason; He gave us a life that includes, experience, long-term thinking, gray hair, age, and much more, for a reason. If we believe, based on our own lives and experience, we are not finished, then we need to listen to ourselves. Period.

Be aggressive if necessary and confront those little bastards who are known as the naysayers. Take hold of those negative people in your life and assess how they have impacted your life. I'm not talking about constructive advice but those people who have taken on the voice of negativity. It doesn't matter the subject, it is just their nature. Remember, it has nothing to do with anything other than their voice, their opinion, which is always the half-empty glass answer.

Sadly, many times their motive is attached to jealousy

or some other limited thinking. Personally, I just resist getting sucked in by keeping a distance. There are enough negative messages out there. Don't be a part of it.

SO-CALLED EXPERTS

If there is anything that I am coming to realize is that the so-called experts are questionable. I have lived through several economic dips and turns, and the only time the "experts" with the right answers emerged was after the fact: the "hind sight" experts.

The Monday Morning financial Wall Street quarterbacks are everywhere. They are our modern-day sleight of hand charlatans. They are the master spin-doctors and they have marketed their BS brilliantly because they have plenty of advertising dollars behind them. They sell their words because they are making a lot of money for a lot of people. I know I'm sounding a little angry, so I'll chill but I don't like people who try to steal our "free will". So there! Just watch out for the brainwash: right, left, or in between.

Trust yourself because that is where God speaks the loudest! If you give up that resource they have won and everyone else loses because it is us—the collective us—that should be the voice of reason, the voice of experience.

For them it's all about marketing, all about the "spin". Their guess was typically no more than a guess in the first place. Be aware of those evil people on TV, or the media who attempt to take away your confidence. They attempt to discredit your own instincts and what you already know to be true…to their agenda and their made-up truth.

We are the last line of defense. It is a thin line, so it takes the best to defend that line, but remember, we are the best and the most qualified. We don't even have to beat them. We just need to be at that line—immovable and steadfast.

Even if we perform the function to our children or grandchildren to take a second look at things, we have accomplished a lot. Let our voice, at least be a voice of caution. I can't tell you how many times I've saved my son from unwanted or reactive purchases. As his father I am careful not to be very critical which allows him to look at his own decision making and not focus on defending himself. This method has created a lot of trust between us.

All of you have accomplished a lot. Whether it is bringing up your family, putting food on the table, worked for a company for thirty-something years, served in the military—all of it is an accomplishment. All of it deserves at least a medal. All of it deserves respect. We know what it takes we lived it. No one else did. No one else walked in your shoes or my shoes. No one else can really judge us, not you, not me. No teenager, twenty-something, thirty-something, forty-something, fifty-something or... Well, you get the point. Have we got that?!

Surely you must see the truth in that. No one has the right to take that away from any of us, and don't let them! PERIOD.

CHAPTER RECAP

- Doing nothing as a senior makes NO sense.

- Uncover your secret "to do" wish list.

- Society without the Elders make NO sense.

- Don't assume your lack of worth.

- God created Elders for a reason.

- Beware of the "spin doctors."

CHAPTER 7

Spirituality

When I googled spirituality, I was amazed to find a definite lack in clarity in its meaning. Yes, there was a common thread, such as non-material, mystical, philosophy, etc., etc. Now, if there were an argument supporting the critics of Google, a lack of a reliable definition for spirituality would be it.

So, with such an open canvas out there, I have decided to add my own shot at the definition. But more important to me as a student of spirituality I find it is a test to see if my spiritual understanding of things mirrors my own spiritual definition.

So here goes:

Spirituality is a philosophy of living a life that is in

perfect harmony with one's soul.

And, now the soul: The soul is the living energy within everyone that is connected directly to the living energy of God.

So, in short, spirituality is the philosophy of knowledge and wisdom of God transmitted to humans through the soul.

I'm sure the critics will add their two cents worth.

The one thing most knowledgeable scholars will agree is that to be a spiritual person it takes a lot of work. It is without a doubt the most challenging work there is. And why not? It is about being in God's classroom and God is our professor if you will. So, there's no slouching here.

Standing at the head of the class, he states his objective and gives the rules he expects us to follow. And, in exchange, he says that those who take on this challenge will absolutely receive riches of all riches. But you will have to work very hard for it. And if you decide to be my student of life, it will be called, "The Spiritual Path".

Of course, that's my spin on it.

The spiritual path is simply living according to the spiritual knowledge of its laws and rules and understanding how to "see" things from a unique perspective known as "elevated consciousness". Sounds very esoteric but it isn't. It really is having the ability to see things with a greater meaning than what it appears to have on the surface.

Because we are blessed to have God's DNA, we also carry the burden or pleasure of always trying to be like him because "man"—his most cherished creation—is his stated prodigy. And that's quite a task.

For a number of years, while in my twenties, I went through therapy. I can't say it was a total waste of time but in looking back, sorry to say, much of it was. Why, you ask?

It was because God was seldom in the picture. How can anyone even conceive to explain *life* and how to live well in it without having God, who created it all, prominently in the equation?

As I defined earlier, the soul is a living energy that is connected directly to the living energy of God inside each one of us. Remember when God said he created "man" in his own image? Well, we know it is impossible to put any dimensional qualities to that statement, so it must mean something different.

My guess is that God was talking about the internal sameness, like what I call having God DNA. If I'm not mistaken there is a fair amount of consensus within the spiritual community to that thought. So, let's say what I am presenting is acceptable to most of you readers, then what? How is this going to help me put the pedal to the metal?!!!

Personally, I find that my soul is the place inside of me where I find real clarity and inspiration. I believe it's the location of our direct connection to the God frequency.

At first, it was a challenge to even connect to its voice, but eventually I found it by knowing what it wasn't.

I knew through my studies and common sense that my soul was only concerned how I, as a human being on this planet, would grow to become more God-like. I know that sounds pretty lofty, and believe me, I have a way to go but at least it gave me a clear road to follow. What is God-like? Like I said, following the spiritual path, so I knew my ego wouldn't get me there.

I concluded that every decision we make is either ego-based, or soul-based. So, when we do things that please the soul, we are living a spiritual life. There are no exceptions, which kind of simplifies things.

It is like they say: "it's the doing" (being proactive) that makes life either a positive experience or a bad B movie. Everything gets affected, every area, whether it's to keep your business running well, or your relationships with your wife, kids, friends, strangers, etc. running well—all depends on *this* choice.

Choosing the soul direction is not so easy. The ego, which is disguised as fear, second thoughts, or doubt, all fight fiercely to keep you from going there. Yes, it feels like a leap of faith at times, because it is. But there is no other way, at least at first.

However, the good news is that no one in history who has committed to this process, has walked away a lesser person, and those who committed for life to a spiritual road, reap rewards beyond their imagination. No one has ever come through and said, "I should never have done this."

The answer to this is simple. Once you get truly into a spiritual life, things start to happen. Your efforts in becoming a better person; sharing more, forgiving more, etc., start to see benefits. Your stress levels decline, and you start to experience how your positive actions make you feel so much better and so much more in control of your life. If you chose to tiptoe through the process, as I did, do so. Doing what the soul wants doesn't happen in a day.

But once you do commit to letting go of non-soul (ego) connections and allow the soul to give you the other true direction, your life will blossom.

Sound easy? Well, we all know it's not! So, why not? You see, God is smart. He knows his people. He knows that he must create obstacles, and certain laws—universal laws. Moses received some of them but there are others as well. "Cause and effect", "everything comes with a price", to name a few. Understanding these universal laws is what spiritual people do and study as I did. Though many are simple and very clear, how many of us still don't screw up? The fact is that we all screw up! Why did God create this impossible road map? The answer to many of us will make a lot of sense. Simply put, it's that we must earn it. It is part of our DNA, God DNA.

Thinking over my own life, what are the most rewarding and life events that have the most meaning? The answer is, those things I had to earn the most. And just to make sure that no one escapes this process, God invented the Devil with his sidekick, the ego. There lies our ultimate challenge and there resides the world of spirituality.

I am a sailor and there is a saying amongst sailors, "You don't learn to sail in calm waters." Get the point? Of course, you do. Living a spiritual life is, in a way, how to live life in its worst conditions, and not only surviving but surviving with a smile like that sea captain who just rounded the Cape in most horrific conditions. He smiles because he knows he did his job well. He comes away with a better appreciation for life and all it offers, including nice weather. He never takes it for granted.

What he really comes away with is experience regarding how he faced the perils of fear, doubt, and uncertainty.

The decisions, facing the fear, connecting to the Almighty—all that somehow becomes a part of his personal fabric, an indelible tattoo of memories embossed in his mind forever—more commonly known as experiences. We are very familiar with experiences. To live a spiritual life is to have all good experiences, all good memories. We learn to make the right decisions for the right reasons.

Having the knowledge, wisdom, and consciousness makes all the difference. The event doesn't change but what does is our view of it.

And thus, the curtain opens to the new stage, the new reality. Did I, the audience, interpret the play correctly—the way it was intended? That is where knowledge, wisdom, and being aware of the consciousness of the play's message comes in. Life is no different. Just like the play, we need to figure out the intent. But in this case, we need to figure out the intent of life and how it makes us better, and even more God-like, more spiritual.

Here are some questions to ask oneself periodically:

1. Define the desires of the soul?
2. Desires of the ego?
3. Paying attention to our own actions?
4. Where has your soul been in your life?
5. Why is your soul so important now?
6. Other people's souls?
7. What does your soul want?
8. Why do bankers need a soul and how are they still bankers?
9. What are the benefits of the planet with a soul consciousness?

Make peace with your soul…understand what that means.

CHAPTER 8

Long-term and Short-term Thinking

L ong-term and short-term thinking are basic tools for life. It may appear obvious because it comes to us automatically but sometimes the obvious can be a great hiding place for even greater discovery.

One day at a time is biblical in nature. According to many religions and spiritual teachings, every new day has its own energy, its own vibe and unique opportunities. I know there are those already rolling their eyes, but you know, hopefully at our age, we are more open to things that don't always make sense on the more rudimentary level.

I do daily meditations. Though it is repetitive in nature, I am still amazed how often I need to be reminded of certain ideas and concepts that have turned bad days into good days, or even eliminating having bad days all together. Some of those are as follows:

1. To thank God for another day.

2. Remember to choose a positive path versus a negative path in any given situation.

3. Try to be more intuitive and trust my instincts.

4. Be more concerned about what is totally in my best interest as a spiritual human being. Some would say: what actions would benefit my soul versus my ego or negative desires.

5. Try not to be judgmental.

6. What is important in a person is their inside—not outside—appearance.

7. Ask God for the strength to fight off the negative situations when they occur.

8. Acknowledge my certainty in following a spiritual path.

9. Reject my reactive impulses and negative behavior.

10. Remember the power of love.

11. Always keep the big picture in mind.

Mind you, I screw up but at least thinking about those concepts on a daily basis has improved my life immensely. It also reminds me how important every personal decision is, whether it's how you talk to a phone solicitor, or how you react to a tricky situation with family and friends. The right choices in these momentary situations can make the difference between a successful and joyful day, or a day you totally want to forget.

It may seem cumbersome at first, but I promise your

effort will pay off in spades when you focus on moment-by-moment choices. Making it a habit is nowhere as difficult as going to the gym, and each right choice you make will provide instant gratification of the good kind. The benefits also include better focus and feeling like you are living life more because you'll see how every moment really does count.

Still, when you think of it, some days are better than others. We all have good and not-so-good days. No great revelation there! But what I've found important is whatever the incident that surfaced is, the spin I give it is what makes all the difference. What was the interpretation I gave to it? Was it a reactive interpretation or a more reasonable one? Did I play being a victim, and that was the reason it was happening?

This dilemma is what finally got me into the world of spirituality. It was there where I found my happiness. Proper long-term and proper short-term thinking was how I got there.

Years of probing, searching, and studying have taught me that much of life's happiness lies in having the right point of view. Spirituality has given me that perspective. The amazing thing is that those answers were literally thousands of years old. Talk about withstanding the test of time!

When I'm in the middle of those bad days and feeling the angst, I keep in mind is that the following day will always be better...without fail. The better may vary from kind-of-better to a whole-lot-better.

Knowing just that truth—that things are better the next day—is huge for me. It diminishes the negative or bad feelings, knowing tomorrow will be a reprieve. It is part of short-term knowledge I rely on without fail. I am not talking about the events themselves but the wisdom I attach to it. Let's call it what people have called it for some time now, being the *Monday night quarterback*. For me it's a way of looking back and recognize where I screwed up so the next time I can do better.

Now let's look more at long-term thinking.

Through the years, I have heard when death comes about, some individuals prepared their eventual passing seamlessly. All estate matters were taken care of and all appropriate papers were filed. On the other side of the coin, I heard where estates were unsettled, and paperwork was a mess, and took years to unravel.

Why that happens is found in underlying issues that, when uncovered, can be deep and laden with anger, resentment, jealousy, payback—you name it. That is where we need to look. Putting aside the pain and suffering this can create to others, in spirituality it is seldom about the other people but rather about you and only you.

Yes, short-term and long-term thinking are not just tools of rational thinking, but they are also great tools for spiritual opportunity. Being happy is all about making the right choices. It's that simple.

Because we are seniors, we know more than any other age group the value in thinking long-term. On the other side of the coin, however, there are times when short-term thinking, or even immediate decisions, need to be made. No matter what anyone says, one needs to have an overview attached to those decisions. What we're talking about is having the ability and the experience to see how these potential decisions flow out over time, even the decisions that are made under duress. Every action has consequences whether it's short-term or long-term thinking, so let's look at that.

For the above reason, I tend to be an environmentalist.

For me, it is important to be a friend to nature. Aside from the scientific community or anyone's political agenda, I try and use my common sense as well. Living in Montana has taught me much about nature and how man's intervention can produce both good and bad results. That is why I tend to attach myself to the indigenous people worldwide and listen to what they have to say. Why, you ask?

To me they are the experts and those who talk the most about long-term thinking. They are also the ones who have claimed nature to be a living and breathing expression of God, and I like that thinking.

I was told their elders commonly try and make decisions that go out at least five generations. Of course, there are those who will find loopholes in my statement, but it is not about that. It is the concept of their thinking. The air, the water, the trees, earth, animals large and small that are all revered as God's creations and has a spiritual attachment that needs to be respected and cared for. That's the side with which I align.

Whether it's short or long-term thinking, the body of those thoughts must be for the greater good—to be in concert with our better self.

When I embrace this thinking, I always know the direction is solid. The benefit of our seniors to know that over all our mistakes in the past we can draw on and remember what *really* worked. Why doubt it?

Always, it is my attempt to help seniors to feel empowered, and I know I can't use a bunch of bull to do it. Everything I say or propose I need to be able to look into the eyes of each and every one you out there, so every word has to come from the real me. After all, if the things I say sound like everyone else, why waste the ink?

CHAPTER RECAP

- As seniors we understand why long term thinking is important.

- Thinking short term also has benefits.

- When has long term thinking failed you?

- Seeing the positive outcome of a long term decision.

- Every action has consequences.

CHAPTER 9

Romance

omance. Finally! OMG we can now talk about why we all came to this party!

So, now that we are either a believer in science reasons, or in God reasons, why give us romance? What practical reason would we need it? Women can't seem to live without it, and men seem to fumble with it. Regardless, think about how our world would be without it. What a void it would create. It would be like removing the very scent from the rose itself.

In thinking about romance long and hard, the obvious conclusion is, I believe everyone needs to find a common ground. Dimming the lights and breaking out some candles at dinner definitely creates a different emotional reaction to us guys than it does to you ladies. On the other side of the coin, how annoying is it to you ladies to hear old reminiscent football stories of the past? Yes, we are very different emotionally, and what conjures up a romantic vibration is also very different. So, the answer please.

Simply, *cooperation and communication*. Ladies, if you really want more of your kind of romance in your relationship you should know *it is possible*. It just takes some work…on *your* part.

The one ingredient that towers above all is the concept of *sharing*. What do I mean by that? Well, to give you a hint, it's not, *what has he or she done for me lately?*" but rather, *What have I've done for he or she lately?* In short, it is the antithesis of selfish behavior. It is all about finding the true joy of giving and more giving.

I can now see the mountains of complaining emails about being a giving person for decades with their spouses being takers and takers. If that's the case, I can only feel sorry for those takers who have never found the true joy of giving. On a personal note, I can only say how joyous it is to me to share with my love ones.

Now mind you, when I'm sharing, it is done from an unconditional place inside of me, so I'm not expecting anything in return. This level of giving is exhilarating. I can only say that those who have never experienced this feeling have missed life at its best. Why, you ask? The answer is both simple and profound…it's because the satisfaction lasts forever.

Now here comes the coup de gras. Just imagine the possibilities if both you and your spouse acquired this mindset of being *sharers*. What if the two of you were dedicated to this concept of unending sharing? Imagine the mindset where "what have you have done for me lately" was non-existent. Shocking concept for many, I know.

If you were only focused on sharing, wow, that would be a biggie.

Okay, so let's start with baby steps instead. Let's start with changing some small habits that fit the description of selfish behavior camouflaged as sharing. I'll just pick one.

An example, if I may. Okay, you come home from your day and your spouse is there. He or she is typically happy to see you. What would be the preferred words coming out from your lips? The answer is, "Hi hon, how are you? How was your day? I hope it was a good one ". Keep it positive and don't fall into... "What a crummy day I had" looking for the sympathy card instead.

Thinking that you are fulfilling your sharing of things by telling your spouse about your day that was fraught with your problems is missing the boat. You are just using the opportunity as an emotional dumping ground for yourself.

That's the secret. In other words, sharing is an enrichment. It is something that becomes an enjoyment for the other person to receive. And yes, it can be as inexpensive as a smile.

In short, proactive sharing means that you are giving, not receiving. This is so important. The act of sharing needs to be defined as a selfless act. And as for you women, us men need to understand that you are different. What appears to be emotional dumping by you is just a download like a computer. It's usually not personal, just a required.

The misconception that men know what you are talking about when it comes to romance is totally false. We men hear it, we see examples of it on T.V., and certainly see it in the movies, but it is as foreign to our DNA as a GI Joe doll is to your DNA. Of course, to generalize only opens the door to objections but allow me leeway this one time.

I am sure many of you women will find that though your partner may be romantic to an accepting level, there is always room for improvement. Not to be too redundant, life is not easy, nor is it supposed to be. Always, the permanent joy in life is to figure it out.

If you ladies say you're just too battle-worn by those recurring and annoying negative comments, or thoughts like, *how could you forget*, or *It would be nice if you could buy some flowers sometimes*, think of the potential rewards of being able to turn all that around.

Here's the key: the window of opportunity is in the fact that men have this very strong male quality of *needing to please*. My point taken when you women may often question why your spouse tends to offer his opinion when just a willing ear is required. A harder confirming argument would be to ask how many years he has taken out the garbage without a verbal complaint!

So, now what? Well, speaking as a man, I put the romance ball back in the court of you women. I do this not to be mean or anything, but because every situation has its uniqueness and key to the solution.

Okay. I'll offer a hint. It's not about what you want, but to include what he "likes" to ignite what you want. I believe this formula would ensure more flowers, candlelit dinners, spontaneous adventures, and an overall sensitivity to the joys of romance in a willing and sincere way. It won't be just an obligation, but something men can connect to and thoroughly enjoy.

Hint #2. Put your man inside the showroom of a Ferrari or classic car dealership. Just be the lookie-loos. Of course, this suggestion will vary.

Watch them conjure up the romantic emotions—even at seventy or older. Observe them as they reconnect to their sense of youth, excitement, adventure, sensuality, and freedom. All very romantic, if you ask me. This can be even more ramped up if you share those moments with him and you fantasize yourself in the passenger seat. That's the key.

The trick is allowing him to put you in his imaginary Ferrari. Right to the "wanting to please" part of his brain, which is laced in romance even you can enjoy.

Share the fantasy and let him show you how cool he can be. Believe me, it will go a long way in turning the fantasy trip to a car dealership to a dozen affordable red roses, a nice dinner, or some other reasonable alternative.

Remember, men have fought duels, battles, and wars to show the power of their need to please a woman. How do we get him to initiate it willingly? This is where you women need to be a little creative and try to find some common ground. I already gave you a few suggestions.

Because men are the admittedly the weak link here, you women must be the proactive ones. In a way our roles may have to be reversed. In the later years, some of you women may have to be a little on the aggressive side…in a feminine aggressive way.

Personally, I like the persuasiveness that you females have. I can't really describe it but you all have it. It's feminine, beautiful, and powerful. As a father to a beautiful teenage girl, I became aware of this—as most all dads with daughters have. At a shockingly early age, women come with a godly talent to get what they want. Bottom line, most men are truly ripe for the taking.

The trick here is that we men think it's all about us and how thoughtful you are. Anyway, I am totally confident you women know what your spouse likes. Well, give it to them! It could as little as playing a classic oldies song you guys shared in earlier years. Lord knows being of our generation we are not short on great music that conjures up heartfelt feelings.

Old photos also open great romantic opportunities. If any of these tend to show your man in a good light, I promise the rewards will unfold before your very eyes.

It's all about touching the heart, the most powerful endeavor on the planet. So, if you can find the romantic button to his heart, you've got it made and he'll be driven to return the favor in spades. Men typically don't need much, but a little compliment, a little ego booster, can go a long way. And when he's ready to return the favor, leave nothing to chance and let him know what you want: flowers, a nice dinner, chocolates, etc., and the kicker will be he'll be happy to do it...really.

Romance is nothing more than a treasure of amazing feelings housed in our heart. And guess who put it there, because it's not there by accident. So, let's open our hearts and enjoy the ride.

THE PARTY POOPER

A special warning: the one component we all have and will pretty much have till the day we die, is our ego. It will kill anything beautiful, especially if we let it. I believe that romance is also a tool to combat our ego. When we feel that romantic feeling, the "me" component takes a backseat to those warm feelings of sharing. Now don't forget!

CHAPTER 10

Becoming the Perfect Lover

S o, in short, romance is food for the soul. And like any food, it has qualities of a variety of colors, smells, and even tastes. Thus, the discovery of wine? :) Just kidding or…maybe not. But the point is that romance is laced with many options and many choices. Be open. Be proactive. Be creative!

Now that we have learned how to create more romance, the next step doesn't require too much of an imagination. Remember God is behind it all…if we are going to do it right. That is why it's not too late to be a great lover. In fact, for some, it couldn't happen until now.

The good news about this subject is that we can pretty much leave behind all those mistakes we made concerning one of God's most important gifts to humanity. We can start anew. Thank God, we can now, for the most part, look at those assorted T.V. commercials, films, and explicit advertising photos, and, with a wry smile, say to oneself how off target they really are. It's amazing how humanity is so susceptible to turning the beauty into the beast—the sacred into a sin. But let's face it, most all of us have our share to repent.

Now that we are more mature and have seen our ways of the past, we can finally look at this from a different light. Maybe because we are so bombarded with *sex* and not the beauty of God's gifts that we are hardly open to the concept of God having anything to do with it. Well, silly, of course he does...just open your eyes and heart to the idea.

In some circles of spirituality, they say that when making love with love it awakens angels and sends beautiful energy into the universe. Even kissing, they say, will send amazing beautiful energy into heaven and beyond. So, go kiss away. Lord knows this universe can use all the positive vibes it can get! That's what I call, an added bonus, so remember the angels are all waiting. So, give a kiss and make the universe happy. No one steal that for a bumper sticker!

Love is one of the most important foods for the soul. And so, it goes, add the soul to the equation and everything changes, and the rewards are heavenly. The soul has no ego, has no agenda, it just wants to be connected to the God-like qualities we all possess, and you have made your soul a happy camper. Add that happiness to sharing in a loving way with your special person and sparks will fly, and you'll come to a glimpse of heaven on earth.

FOR THOSE SENIOR SINGLES

For those who are living the single life, I have a few suggestions that might guide you in reconnecting to the opposite sex. You'll find it is so much easier when you apply a few rules.

Rules of engagement for men

1. Sharing is very effective. It takes you out of feeling creepy.
2. Most women like interesting stories.
3. They like confidence.
4. They love funny, even stupid jokes.
5. Keep it light.
6. Share a story or even a problem. Allow them to offer a solution.
7. Be playful.
8. Don't be cliché.
9. You won't get lucky, but their energy will light up great fires within, which are more lasting.
10. Girls are fickle. If they blow you off one day, they can love you the next. So, don't take it personally.
11. It's fun.
12. Don't get over-confident. Play it cool. Always!
13. We are making friends, not looking to get lucky.

Rules of engagement for women

1. Feel your power of loving kindness and nurturing.
2. Ask meaningful questions.
3. Teach them about a women's point of view, even some secrets.
4. Just let the conversations flow and help him out.
5. This is not a date. It's about connecting to male energy in an enjoyable way.
6. Remember, we are making friends, not lovers.

All you need to know about women for you guys, and what you need to know about men for you ladies, is probably the most fun part of this chapter for me. To me God's message is that life is not simple. Why else did he create women?

A guide you might think of when you are with women:

1. Appreciate our differences.
   A. they are guided mostly by their emotions.
   B. they have their secrets.
   C. they have internal dialogue.
2. Being pretty for them is important.
3. They like complements.
4. Flowers always work.
5. How to make a connection.
6. What women like: stories, romance, etc.

All about men:

1. We like to please.
2. We like to solve problems.
3. We like this simple, bottom-line approach to life and its problems.
4. Conquerors.
5. Want to be a little bit or a lot like a bad boy.
6. Frightened by women's power.
7. Fear of rejection.

My intent is to merely open the door for more thought and encourage more action. And that is the key: more action. Please everyone. Let go of this fear of rejection. I promise you "fear" is NOT your friend. If rejection does come, so what! You're only diminishing your ego, and that's a plus. But if you do reach out of your comfort zone and something does happen, wow, what a great reward.

CHAPTER 11

Think Healthy it's Simple

At least for me. Don't be jealous because I will share with you how simple it is. My son Anton is a health nut. Mind you, I am happy for it.

One of the things I put at the very top of the "healthy" list is medicine that doesn't come out of a bottle, and the cost is free. The first such medicine is called "appreciation".

It feels good when I appreciate things; feeling good is great medicine. Like I said, it costs nothing, and I can take this medicine anytime anywhere. Another medicine is sharing. Again, I can do it almost anywhere, anytime. Yes, it can cost if I share in a way of a donation, and because it does cost something, it makes it an even stronger medicine.

Some may challenge this theory, but even science now

points to the negative effects of negative emotions such as stress and anger as being the number one reason for health issues. So, why shouldn't positive emotions or feelings be also medicinal?

The problem, of course, is that Madison Avenue knows this, but they are all about the money. They try and convince us that the good free medicine we get from God and his perfect nature is worthless. Instead, they attach every bad chemical, food, and drink, and make them "manmade" and taste good with tons of sugar. Isn't it a wonder why we hear every now and then how these manmade products do, in fact, eventually kill us?

Of course, I am perhaps overstating the point but over the years I have found natural remedies for high blood pressure, high sugar levels, being overweight, skin sores, and even toothaches. I even was cured from a herniated disc years ago though the back surgeons were lining up at the door. The cost? Almost nothing.

Madison Avenue trickery is not very nice, and certainly not very spiritual. They take this "good feeling" like fresh air and water—which is also a present from God—and steal it for their own diabolical purpose. They even redefined God's "good feeling" to what really amounts to the feeling of what causes addiction. Life is tricky business. But hey! We are the seniors, the elders. We know. We probably even invented some of those schemes.

I remember several years ago in Montana, I was involved in a group of Blackfeet Indians who set up a nonprofit company to preserve and protect the purity of the Spanish mustang horse. It was a great program and I made several friends who remain very dear to my heart. One such person, Larry, came to my house. We took a walk on the property along with Anton by his side.

I stayed close, eager to hear his words to my son. "You see", Larry said, "most people just walk around looking at the birds and the sky and innocently look around blindly. But I look at the plants on the ground and say, there is Nica Nickie plant—a good medicine for headaches. If you rub it on a cut it will help heal it. Did you know, this here plant will help if you have an upset stomach?"

Wow, how amazing. Needless to say, it was a wonderful afternoon. He turned this simple walk in the fresh air (also medicine) into a memory I will always cherish. My son may have been very young at the time, but I am sure somewhere in his consciousness, it is still all there.

It was a great lesson my friend Larry gave to me and my son, on how God provides. We just need to be shown. The interesting thing is the possible cures yet to be discovered within nature.

I have been involved in the alternative medicine world for most of my life. Even my mother believed in having fresh vegetables (never canned) with every meal. She even warned us against sugar. Imagine way back then! So, it was through her influence that I became aware of the benefits of the kind of food I put in my body. Perhaps it was her influence that I became a big advocate of organically grown food. I just instinctively feel better knowing that the food I eat, and my family eats, is pesticide free for the most part, and is a non-gmo product. I am sure there is some scientific blah, blah that would try and convince me otherwise but why should I rely on that? I would rather be safe than sorry. Let their science stand the test of time as the natural foods have. I can wait.

In short, what goes into my body is important to me. Now mind you, I'm not perfect, and Lord knows I've strayed. But it is the rare exception and not the norm. To me, that's what important. I do what I can and not to be too neurotic except when it comes to some things like any kind of soda. That is something I will never put in my system.

A little about being physical. I have been an athlete most of my life. For me it works. I'm not the guy who has worked out consistently for forty or fifty years. The fact is that I may do nothing for several years but then, somehow something inside awakens and pushes the "get your butt going" button. I don't know how many times I've stopped and got going again.

In fact, I have a friend—one of those people who always worked out—laugh at me. "Oh yeah, starting up again?" He adds his wry, sarcastic smile. "Yup, I would say," with a tinge of embarrassment. But what I learned along the way has been very valuable. The trick for me is to shed that adage, "No pain, no gain" to go easy as long as you can, and your body will tell you to increase your efforts when it's ready.

I don't know how many times that has worked for me. After fifteen years of much discomfort, I recently had my knee replaced. I did the required physical therapy and yes, that was a bitch, but when I was finally on my own, I continued to bike at a gym for a month or two. I even worked out with some upper body machines. I was feeling pretty top rated. All this at sixty-nine years old.

I'm not bragging, (maybe a bit) but the interesting thing is that "muscle memory" kicked in. We're talking about awakening ten years of sleepy time, ten years of cobwebs on muscles! I cannot impress you enough how amazed I was to feel those old feelings, in "my" body.

There was a period in my life, maybe some twenty years ago I began to jog. I lived at the beach in L.A., so the location was perfect. Off I went. I've never been the skinny type but in this period in my life, being "almost" skinny was almost in sight.

However, fast forward...I ran thirteen miles every other day after two to three years. Man, was I the man! I was in love with jogging. It was not a jog to me but an adventure. I explored streets I would never venture, and when I traveled, jogging was my preferred mode of transportation. Everything became up close and personal. It was great, and I felt great. But like most wonderful things—at least in my life—things change. I can't even remember what happened.... Oh yeah, now I remember, it was a woman.

The one thing I failed to mention about starting and re-starting a physical regime was that when I could afford it I hired a trainer to get me on track and going again with no excuses. I can't tell you how appreciative I am to have had them in my life. Again, I don't know what each and everyone's situation is but if you can afford it I would recommend a nice young trainer who promises to go easy for you and get you going again. Not with the end goal to do a marathon but to get things going again. Enough said.

It may sound strange but another way to think healthy is through prayer. Prayer, as discussed in another chapter, is medicine. Throughout history stories of amazing examples of medical miracles have been recorded and certainly in modern times, the papers feature these kinds of miracles almost daily...and those are only the big miracles. I would bet that almost everyone has some experience in some kind of medical miracle, large or small.

So, if you add them all up, it must be in the millions of millions. The problem is that because it is so frequent, and Madison Avenue is not selling it, we just take it for granted.

We've been programmed to believe that unless it's a

big medical miracle we have become unappreciative and, thus, diminished its value. It is, in fact, such a common part if our "positive" internal dialogue that it is another automatic gift from God.

But the fact is, behind every medical miracle, there lies a prayer, whether it's a conscious one or a subconscious one...an outward one or an internal one. And even those prayers done by people you didn't know: mothers, fathers, sisters, brothers, friends, etc. who might have prayed for you without your knowledge.

To conclude this chapter, I just wanted to open your eyes that there is so much more medicine out there that doesn't come from a doctor's prescription. In fact, almost every drug has some natural plant- or root-inherent properties at its base. What they don't tell you is that anything "natural", and not the food company's definition of natural, cannot be copy written. So, they add a manmade component to it, so it can be copy written.

Your attorneys know what I'm talking about.

A few notes about thinking healthy:

1. Do it for your grand kids, wife, etc.
2. Make it a mindset.
3. Communicate with other healthy people.
4. Don't focus on your health issues.
5. Pray for a cure.
6. Be persistent.

Our body has trillions of cells that are on your side. They fight for you every day. They have a singular mindset, and that is to fight till the death for you, so help them out.

Alternative medicine vs. western medicine is a wide topic for me to discuss because I have been a big supporter of alternative medicine for most of my life…and for me it has greatly paid off. There is so much data out there, pro and con:

1. Medicine today: pills, pills, and more pills.

2. Trust your instincts.

3. Do your research.

4. Today, a lot of traditional doctors are more open to alternative medicine.

5. Choices I've made.

6. Never give up.

CHAPTER 12

Friends and Family

Are a mystery to me. When I look at that part of my life and its importance, it's almost like figuring out the most complex question of the human species. Let me break it down, Sandy style....

Where lies our biggest disappointments, tons of emotional history, biggest highs, biggest lows, anxieties, trust, distrust, making up, breaking up...on and on and on...and so on?! It's exhausting!

To find the truth, and the answers to it all, it lies within the spiritual world.

And within the spiritual world I am sure at our stage in the game you've heard of "Unconditional Love". Once again, this concept can conjure up the spectrum of emotions. And remember, much of this book relies on spiritual wisdom, thank God. But I want to break it down friend by friend, family member by family member, enemy by enemy. If we can get to a place of an eternal peace with all of them, then the price of admission for this book was well worth it. So here we go…

We all have had our share of friends, foes, and in-between. Some bring up good memories, bad distasteful memories, and some are somewhat wishful memories, and the entire gamut in the middle. I have a little story of a long-lost friend from a junior high school vintage I'd like to share. It's an example of the way life goes sometimes. It is also an example of how the "soul" has a life of its own, void of time, space, and motion.

This story has its beginnings back some fifty-plus years ago. Like any good story, there was this girl (a beautiful girl in her early teens) and a young, good-looking jock. Unlike most jocks, (actually me) he was tough on the outside but a soft, sensitive romantic on the inside.

She had a beautiful rounded face, dark hair, sparkling dark eyes, perfect white skin. Her looks could have inspired the images of Snow White herself. Along with an innocent aura, it gave her top rated marks in that junior high school girl pool.

I'm not going to detail the "how it happened" part of the story, at least for now, but what's important is that we struck up a friendship over the phone many years later. It was an East Coast/West Coast thing. It was honestly a little rough going in the beginning, but I was persistent. Why, you may ask. I'll defer that question and answer to the cosmos. But we eventually started to talk and talk and talk. That shy, beautiful teenager was no longer shy, though her beauty was still very much visible.

As the comfort level settled in with this new friend, she said, "Sandy, I do have a confession." I was clueless to what it could possibly be. Then she added, "Do you remember that we went out on those two dates?" Sorry, but I was dumbfounded!

"Are you serious?" I said. How in the world could I have forgotten that? I went out twice with little-miss-dream-girl but I had no memory of it. Amazing. But hold on, it gets better. So, she continues on the phone, and I know she must be smiling to herself by now and says, "And you know what? We kissed…and you were my first ever kiss!" My jaw literally dropped.

OMG, as they say. You know guys, I'm sorry but this is a legitimate moment I will always treasure, though I don't remember a damn thing about it, I will hold on to that "bragging right" story till the last breath.

I'm not telling you this story to create some jealousy out there, but to remind all of you—and I mean this—is that we never know who we affect, whether in a positive or negative way, in our lives.

Her story was a big wake up call for me. Think of all those little secrets we had back then. How nice it would be if we had the opportunity to reveal them all. Think of how it would feel to openly say, "Hey, I'm sorry for acting the way I did back then or said the things I said to you."

Well, according to the spiritual community, you can.

The way it's done is to conjure up as many as you remember. Get them in your mind and with the utmost sincerity, say, "I'm sorry." Or say, "Thank you." Either way, it's legitimate. I promise, you'll feel the difference.

Every person you encounter is there for a reason. Every person, relative, (including moms, dads, and children) was put in your life to teach you, and them, something.

Yes, it's very personal. Mark my words, it's true. The more uncomfortable they are, or were, the bigger the reason.

Make peace with them. No matter how hard, kill your pride, stifle your ego, and make peace. You will love me for it.

Family...*oy vey*! Look, if you think I'm going to be rational here, forget it! Personally, just writing that word conjured up every emotion under the sun.

Instead of writing a narrative, I've decided to make a list of points I've learned along the way. You may not agree with this list, but I am presenting it nevertheless. I truly live by this list, and all I can say is that it has given me much peace.

1. God set up your family.
2. The formula of life.
3. Karma; they chose you and you chose them.
4. They are our teachers, and the reverse is also true.
5. Always teach your kids from a place of love...always, no matter what.
6. Teach your family love.
7. Teach your family compassion.
8. Keep your ego out of family business.
9. Sometimes being right is the booby prize.
10. Be a great listener.
11. Never too late to forgive.
12. Never too late to correct your mistakes.
13. Never too late to ask for forgiveness.
14. Allow your family to live their own lives without judgments.

15. Encouragement goes so much further than preaching.

So, take this list and hopefully it will bring some peace. Again, life is a puzzle and being happy is the prize...

CHAPTER 13

The Universe is Working for our Highest and Greatest Good

Erase the past. Are you thoroughly confused?? Well, I don't blame you.

A few chapters prior, you read how you are the witness and participant of history and the value of it, and now am I saying to forget all? What!? The answer is…no.

What I am saying is that there are things in our own past, or our own baggage, our own sins, our transgressions. Go to the nearest church, temple, or person if they are still alive, confess it all. Each religion or spiritual teaching has the avenue to repent to say you're sorry, to say you screwed up, and "I'm sorry and I will never do it again". Hold your hand over your heart while saying it.

It is a burden, a weight we all carry, and if we are to

move ahead, to move freely, we need to release the part of the past that has stayed tied to us like an emotional anchor.

You may not be able to cleanse yourself completely, and maybe you are not supposed to, but the more you can do, the freer you will become.

Redemption. According to most, if not in all spiritual teachings, honest repentance is more powerful than we know. Why? It's because we are really asking God to forgive us...and if we are sincere, he always listens.

My dad, with whom I honestly didn't have a great relationship, left me with this morsel. His quote was: "He who travels lightest, travels fastest." Whether he was speaking from a physical or emotional point of view, or if we give him the kudos in its duality, the point is, whatever we can come to terms with, emotionally or spiritually, the lighter we get and the faster, freer, and happier we become.

At our age, the goal is to become as slim and trim as possible, shedding as much negative energy as possible. To follow my father's advice, let's follow the duality of his words of wisdom and lose a few negative pounds as well. This is something we *all* can do. Let us take charge again. We are seasoned players, "the" seasoned players.

One more point to mention; The more we open up and work on ourselves, it allows more room for God to enter. They call that our vessel. The bigger the vessel, the more we can take in God's energy...and that's when spiritual miracles happen.

CHAPTER 14

Retirement is like a Double-Edged Sword

For some it is the door to freedom and others it is the door to the cemetery. Retirement can create so much pent-up anticipation that it can wreak emotional havoc when this new reality sets in.

The imagination conjures up things like sandy beaches, green golf courses, pina coladas, even throwing away the alarm clock. The sky's the limit regarding this final chapter of life, and the hope of how amazingly happy I'm going to be.

What's that saying? The road to hell is paved with good intentions? Hey! I'm not here to give you a ticket to the Mississippi Blues Train, but instead to keep you from getting on board!

So, let's take a breath and face this new door to your finest hours.

The great advantage we have is experience, which tells us we need to be realistic. What life has also taught us is that sometimes we need a plan...a realistic plan, and an important part of that plan should include ample time for decompression.

When your body and mind have been on automatic for all those years, a major re-boot is necessary. Make it a time for you to look at this period as a rebirth. Clear the slate.

Another door is about to open so keep your mind open as well. Inject your mind with hope, opportunity, a smile, and a positive attitude. By reading this book, your new life, a new chapter in your life has the potential to be the best years in your life. That is what I promise if you do the work. Yes, you're going back to work. But this time you're the absolute boss who's in control.

Speaking from experience, my new careers as a teacher and writer came to me. Yes, I did use logic in my decision to move forward with both those choices, but my heart was also very much included in the process. And as I look back, I recall some nervousness but overall my inner self told me to move forward, and so I did. I honestly can say that my biggest enemy was the negative thoughts. But more important, those negative thoughts turned out to be absolutely and totally inconsequential to the outcome.

So, here I was at seventy starting several new ventures while almost totally broke! These are things I've never ever done before. Yes, it takes work. And yes, it was a challenge but what fueled me was "desire". For the first time, I was secure enough within me to follow my heart. That was the key for me. That became my fuel...a renewable source of energy that reaches out to the universe.

Sounds lofty? So what! It's true.

You just need to discover the kind of work that connects to your heart. It will put smiles on your face and give a wonderful reason to get up in the morning. Every day will be precious. Believe it or not, you will have a love affair with work. It's an amazing feeling.

When one thinks about all the possibilities, it is truly endless. Even if you have physical issues, the possibilities are still endless.

I saw something on the internet about this guy who has no hands, no feet to speak of, and is a motivational speaker and *drummer*! My heart aches from so much love I have for this person. His energy, his spiritual energy, is so beyond words. I am sure every day for him is not always peaches and cream, but I know his spiritual tools are amazing.

Think of him as the captain I spoke about in the earlier chapters and think how this man is immersed in the most difficult hurricane conditions and still living strong. How? It's because he has found that his heart and his mindset are his best assets that conquers all.

Simply, retiring is time for you to reassess. This is a new slate, a new you to an open door.

Your tools from your senior life experiences are very powerful. If you can combine those valued experiences with a new proper mindset that connects to the heart, you are truly off to the races. But mind you, I'm not telling you to head straight to your local horse track!

We know, in all honesty the world has its issues, and much of it is because they have taken us seniors out of the equation on purpose. Why, you ask? The simple answer is because we are the experts of common sense. Test my theory the next time you go shopping with a grand child who wants to buy everything in the store. Basically, we are bad for the economy. But on the other side of the coin, good for teaching our grandchildren some discipline.

I am not reinventing the wheel but getting back to what humanity has known from the start, and that is the value of the senior or the elders' input.

It is part of God's design that we acquire our experiences, knowledge, and wisdom and do something positive with it. God is not stupid, and there is nothing He has created—and I mean nothing—that doesn't have a purpose, including *you*. You just need to honestly look for it and it will come—another universal law.

At our age, we are continually receiving notices of old friends and relatives who have passed away. I have written many words of sadness to commemorate their path back to heaven. Honestly and personally, the voice that is always present within me is, *Thank God this is not me.* Every time, without fail, I am scared. I am scared that I will go without finishing my business on earth this time around.

When the dust settles, I go into deep appreciation for everything. It is an amazing wakeup call that I want to share with all of you—those who are reading this book, those who have read this book, those who will read my book, and of course for all those who will never read this book—to find inspiration. Take this time we have left and make it count.

It is with my entire heart and soul that I reach out to those elders who are either calling it quits, giving up, or losing faith. Ask yourself why you are still amongst us. God can take you at any time, at any place, but so far, he hasn't.

Take advantage of that. I am, in my humble way, asking you who are now traveling a new road of retirement, to take advantage of it in the best conceivable way. Hopefully, I can help with some suggestions, tricks, anything that will get your motors revving again because those revs are still in us somewhere, and if you find them you'll see and feel how sweet they are. Volunteering, by the way, is very powerful, and it puts you with good people.

Suggestions:

1. non-profits
2. ecology
3. health
4. hospitals
5. mentoring
6. political parties
7. volunteer at schools
8. libraries
9. zoos
10. animal organizations
11. Red Cross
12. Salvation Army
13. church/synagogues
14. youth groups
15. youth athletic teams
16. board of directors

This list is only there to stimulate your juices. The surprising thing I found repeatedly, is that being a senior has the power to open doors that were shut in your past. Please take advantage of that.

"Little Big Man," with Dustin Hoffman, is one of my all-time favorite films. I remember seeing it for the first time in the Grauman's Chinese Theatre in Hollywood, California. I was in my twenties and working as an independent film producer with my cousin's husband, Paul. I remember how that movie solidified my new life direction. It somehow identified so many of my inner feelings about the world, people, injustice, justice, the duality of it all, and mostly, the relationship between Hoffman's character and his adopted grandfather, played by Chief Dan George. For a film to have such a positive impact on my life, I am convinced it had a connection to my soul, and I am forever grateful. It showed me that my internal beliefs, though not mainstream, existed, and that I wasn't alone. I think that this understanding, for some reason, gets underplayed in our culture. Trusting one's instincts gets plenty of play on Disney shows but when it gets to the adult world, it somehow disappears.

Yet, when the real leaders and great entrepreneurs of our generation get to express their opinions on life, this becomes the most important part of the message. Yet, to speak it goes back to trusting yourself and understand that mistakes are part of the process. But to get back to the central focus of this chapter, who else is more qualified to speak about this fact of life? Experience is king.

Lately, I have volunteered at my son's public school and lent my time in a classroom of seniors and helped put together a video presentation they were required to do. I can't begin to tell you how fulfilling it was. When these upper teens saw I had something valuable to say, they immediately made an attachment, and were very open to my words. It also gave me an insight as to where they were at maturity-wise and world-wise. I saw how much guidance they needed.

Now, mind you, this is not a criticism, but it was an

observation about a void in a generation that truly needed my input and knowledge. I must say, to their teacher's credit, he was grateful for my words and pointed out that it was very helpful for someone like myself to add to their experience in stepping out into the world.

What I found myself doing was becoming a storyteller, kind of like in "Little Big Man".

Little big man... "Yes, Grandfather."

1. Who else has your wisdom?
2. There is a built-in genetic code that allows for the relationship.
3. Don't take it lightly...it's our most powerful asset.
4. Stories are a great form of teaching.
5. Become familiar with some of the universal truths.
6. Be grateful/appreciate the opportunity.
7. Remember flexibilities.
8. Create your own style.
9. Connect to the power of love especially when it comes to correction.
10. Never get angry.
11. Share your view of the big picture.

Stayk

CHAPTER 15

Change of Heart

There is more and more talk about the "heart". It seems to be a topic among healers, holistic, and even conventional medical establishments that is on the top of the list for discussion, and for a myriad of reasons.

I have heard everything. I've heard about its frequency vibrations to its importance in healing all the other organs. I recently heard that the heart is also a vessel for the receiving and giving of information, even more than one's brain. Go figure.

And how about the heart's spiritual importance? How often have we heard in song, literature, and cinema the effects of the heart...the importance of the heart?

As a senior, the heart has been a growing part of my

life in so many ways. But honestly and sadly, in the past I may have taken it for granted.

One of the more amazing side-effects of becoming a senior: there appears to be a more awareness of the heart. Personally, I have found that I am now constantly checking on my heart, how it's feeling and how certain people affect it. Even in business, it is the heart that is taking over more and more in my decision-making process. My question to myself is, will this action create heart-positive feelings or not?

Can this be another proof of God's work? I am sure this idea is not unique; it might be the most talked about topic throughout the ages. So, what do I have to bring to the table? Have I stumbled onto a new insight, or am I rehashing what has been already expressed? I'll let you decide, and I'm sure you'll let me know.

What I know is that the heart is still an unknown. We dance around what is does, what it says, what it wants, and what it doesn't want. It speaks, it cries, it hurts, it sings, it feels good, feels bad, loves, and it also can be silent. Wow! No wonder science is mystified by it all, and if I could guess, they will probably never be able to put their arms around it. Maybe that's a very good thing.

So, now what?

OK then, here is my thinking. We have the heart on one side, and unlike all other organs in the body, except the brain of course, it needs a voice to express itself. Then here comes the mind. Surely God knew that the heart alone wasn't enough. Yes, the mind is not scrubbed totally. It has been the most important internal measurement of almost everything I do or say. When I was younger, it was the thought that controlled my behavior, now I find it is the heart.

One example of that is if I screw up with my kids. If my son and I ever go to sleep upset with each other, my heart truly aches. I know his heart aches, too. And as we wake up, the first and only thought in my mind and heart is to say I'm sorry to him. If you remember, apparently it is the same for him because it is exactly what he confesses to as well. *Voila!* All is well again. My heart is at peace. His heart is at peace. Life is good! I can't imagine how this same situation would get resolved if I used logic.

I don't really believe there is little difference in the real world. Let's go to a list of corporate heads that have broken the law or their corporate position to destroy people and the land or resources we have on earth. Let's look at the list of politicians or country leaders who have acted in evil ways, to the detriment of their own people and our God-given resources such as water, and even the air that we breathe. What about their hearts?

I believe, contrary to some people's belief, that no one escapes punishment from doing bad things.

What we need to keep in mind: it's not the corporations or the individual governments, or even the institutions, but the people hiding behind the fancy logos. They are people who have mothers, fathers, brothers, sisters, friends, cousins, sons, daughters, and grandchildren. Why is all this important? Because it is people, not companies, corporations, or governments who are making these decisions. There is a person, male or female, behind every desk. Each one making decisions that will create actions, positive or negative.

Take the big picture of all those people and imagine just one thing. Imagine they all decided to check their hearts first before they put their initials to the paper. Yes, imagine if they all put their hand to their heart and asked if what they were about to put into motion was heart friendly or not. Imagine what the outcome would, or could, be.

Now, I don't want to argue this point or put it out for debate because it opens the door to too much chaotic responses. But, me, Sandy Horowitz will tell you in the long run this world would heal and be more productive.

And just for argument sake, what if only 20% of them took notice and decided to follow their heart. What a massive change would take place. Now think of 30%, 40%, 60%, 80%, or 100% who now would decide to follow their heart. Have we found heaven on earth yet? I think we have.

Don't you believe that a campaign to change their hearts might have a better chance of success than pitting lawyer against lawyer, gun barrel against gun barrel? In my opinion, this should be our new social mantra, our new social revolution. Have they followed their heart??? Because we all have a heart, we would know if they were lying or not.

According to every spiritual leader of any consequence, the heart never lies, never proves wrong. It is the ego that only and forever proves to be wrong.

Here we are, indignant, and possibly a little self-righteous on the sidelines scowling at those people. Now is the time to see our own reflection in the mirror. How do we, individually and collectively, measure up to this new mantra of connecting to our heart and rearranging our decision-making to heart-decision-making? What if we lead the charge...show the way? Who best out there is better to be the leaders of "the decisions from heart" movement than us?

1. We can be the judge of their sincerity.
2. Campaign against ego decisions.

3. Show the economic sense.
4. Point out leaders and CEOs who are from the heart.
5. Teach the difference.
6. Show results.

CHAPTER 16

The Second Chance

The subject of this chapter, "The Second Chance" can be a ticket for many to heal a wound that's been there for many years.

The process for mankind is hardly ever easy. No matter how we try, inevitably it is the hard lesson that seems to be our proven path for self-discovery. But if we know this, and accept the process, it becomes easier every time. That's the good news. God, in his infinite wisdom, created this system of pain, sorrow, and tears only to overcome it and having a second chance is a part of that process.

These areas of difficult emotions, if looked at from a healing perspective, can also lead us to a place of happiness and true fulfillment using the heart as the instrument to gauge it all.

I sometimes wince at the attempt of science to decipher this system with tons of verbiage and no mention of God. It's like they attempt to avoid the word God, like it's totally not connected to the human condition.

To fully benefit from what I say, we need to focus on the previous chapter and check the heart and feel the pain of any unresolved situations in our past. For some, I am sure the list may be daunting, and for others it will be somewhat less. But either way, the most effective approach is to start with a written list of people you've hurt, been hurt by, unpleasant words that were said, etc. No one is innocent.

Not so long ago, my friend and I had a tiff. I wrestled with my position in the argument though I qualified it with boasting about my long years of experience in the matter. What I struggled with was the angst it created for my friend. Yes, she held on to her ego as well, but honestly, I was better prepared, and she took the brunt of the emotional fallout. So, what was really accomplished? At the end of the phone call, all I could think of, and feel, was the damage it created to that person's heart…and mine. Right or wrong, I concluded, it was just our egos doing the negative dance.

Thus, the doorway to what this chapter is all about. After all, what did we do wrong, what needed correction? Couldn't I just move on and chalk this down as another bad encounter, just like days of old? Of course, but being a senior somehow changes things. At least it did for me. I didn't want to let it go thinking time would heal it. Why? Because I know from experience, it never does really heal. Amazingly, the heart never forgets; that's part of its job.

As a teacher in grade school, I am often confronted

with little kids and their disputes. The interesting thing is that what I have found to be the most effective and lasting approach is for each kid to say they are sorry regardless of who's at fault. No "one" person is ever at fault, and somehow instinctively these kids know it because I seldom get too much resistance. I would have them put their hand on their heart and ask them if that made them feel better. They always say, "Yes."

Back to the second chance. The key to that door is simply the heart. The moment you rationalize in your mind and reexamine and justify your actions in the past, you are dead meat. Let it go. Put your hand on your heart just like I make those kids do, and say," I'm sorry", *and mean it*. Even if that person is no longer among the living.

The key, however, is to shift that emotional place inside to a place closer to the heart. The defenses, the issues, all seem to fade to where we can see the big picture and what is important. The amazing thing is that the lesson, or point of contention, now appears unimportant. The difference is that our hearts can see the clarity of the issues. Once that happens, we can always revisit.

The important lesson is that we both changed our positions. Once a shift is made the door opens and a second chance unfolds. The interesting thing is that *time* is irrelevant. Whether it's a moment, an hour, day, week` or thirty years, it doesn't matter. Neither do the situations matter. It can be between your boss, your lover, brother, mother, friend, etc.

Although we are always given a second chance, the big caveat is that we can't be in the same internal place as we were the first go-round. We must make a change in our position. If we come to the awareness that there is no right or wrong, and that we have grown as a person, then the door will open. It is not about the other person. We are in charge to change it. I promise.

The second chance covers a lot of personal territory. We are talking about old friends or foes. We are talking about family members. We are talking about bumping into someone on the street.

And the real troublemaker that got us into this mess is usually one's ego and reactive behavior. So, let go of that emotional anchor that only serves our ego. Fess up and say you're sorry. It's magic that gets magical results!

CHAPTER 17

Be Your own Hollywood Producer, writer, Director

You're home relaxing by the TV and the phone rings. "Hello?" the voice says, "are you Mr. Smith?" "Yes," you reply. You think this must be another annoying solicitation. "Well, Mr. Smith, God asked me to call." "I beg your pardon?" you respond. "Well, yes, and I've been sent to you to produce a movie."

Now you know this guy is truly crazy, but just as you're about to hang up, your TV flickers and an image appears. It speaks the words precisely as the ones you are hearing over the phone. "What the heck!"

What I'm about to tell you is that is *all* true. The only stipulation is that you need to believe it and be brave enough to do it.

Personally, this is what I do.

I know for me to improve my day, week, or year I must do some things differently. I must look at myself as clearly as possible. I'm trying to rewrite my character, Sanford (Sandy) J. Horowitz. Now that's fine but how does one do that?

Here are a few hints:

1. What it takes to be a producer. Look at the big picture and create an image of that new you, and see how it can be improved, even a little bit.

2. What it takes to be a writer. Stay away from clichés. Be creative/think outside the box. Make outlines, writing is rewriting. Think about it as much as possible, even while driving, on a train, a plane, or watching commercials.

3. Directing… Stay close to your vision and try not to be derailed.

4. Edit your film and be aware of always moving the story forward TO A POSITIVE RESULT.

5. Put it out there.

So, there you go, off to Hollywood!

CHAPTER 18

Making a Difference is Our Mission Here on Earth

The misinformation about this is that people think that if you have not personally changed the world, it doesn't count. This couldn't be further from the truth. The universe is so complex, so beyond our comprehension, you must be careful about believing some of those clichés out there. Some elevated souls and progressive scientists have discovered that even the smallest incident can have major effects. They even gave it a name "the butterfly effect".

Think of a snowflake or that one drop of water that tipped the scales of the pending avalanche, or the leaky pipe in your house. It's not only the little things that count but the tiny, tiny things as well. A splendid example of this I personally love comes from the animated movie, "Ice

Age". Rent it and you'll see what I mean. You'll also enjoy a little entertainment as well.

The point is that on our own personal level this gives us unlimited opportunities to make a difference. This concept has finally become an indisputable scientific and spiritual coexisting fact that everything affects everything else to one degree or another. It is called quantum physics.

We are discovering that one act of kindness or good deed can cause unseen results. Unfortunately, the opposite is also true about negative actions and negative results. The truth is that a smile to someone can be the one thing that person really needed to get out of a bad mood…and getting out of that bad mood led to that same person giving a little extra to that waitress who happened to need that little extra money for the bus. It sounds somewhat overstated, but it really isn't. This is truly the way our world works.

If you can take this to heart, you will be amazed how much of a difference and effect you are making on your immediate world, and, according to the spiritual world, the universe as well.

Think about it…if you are still breathing, you can affect the universe. Remember, we carry the DNA of God, so anything is possible. Only your negative side of your mind will come up with unending limitations. Yes, I cannot run a four-minute mile, but so what. To me what is important is what I *can* do.

I can still hold a conversation with my kids, friends, or foe, put a few cohesive sentences together, and be an effective teacher. And that is the very short list. Don't take this as a bragging list because I'm sure anyone of you has your own list. Embrace your list and use it to build on. Use that list as emotional food to encourage you.

Throughout this book, a central theme is the

understanding and acknowledgement that there is a negative inclination. And, throughout this book I repeatedly state to recognize those negative inclinations as an enemy…pure and simple. At a certain point, I always face that voice when I'm on a journey. It comes right after I'm feeling good and very enthused. I have checked it out and I know it is the right direction to take but lo and behold, here it comes…the voice that says it's too hard, too time-consuming, too this, too that.

The solution? Simply move ahead. Move forward. I promise you will not die a horrible death. Of course, we're not talking about bungee cord jumping. At least *I'm* not. Just let go and forge forward. This is where "miracles" happen.

The advantage of what I'm saying can be found by going back to the title of this chapter: Making a Difference.

When a person has the right motives and is doing something for the right reasons they have a built-in guardian angel. Perhaps some of you have already experienced this. It's true. Things typically will not be handed to you on a silver platter, but that's not how things of value really work anyway. For me, to become a good teacher took work, but I did it and the results are far reaching.

Another thing about "inspiration" is that when I get these inspirations, they usually occur naturally. What I mean by that is, it will come to me…and not the other way around. Yes, I may be thinking of a new direction, but I don't run towards it. I am patient and wait for it to come to me and when it comes, it has an electric feeling. My entire body feels the buzz.

Being inspired is probably the most satisfying feeling a person can have, especially if it has the earmarks of helping and sharing for others to benefit. As seniors, we are at a great position to connect to this because of our experience in life itself. At our point in life, it is much easier to determine whether we are going off in a direction to satisfy our own selfish desires, or if we're going off in a more satisfying direction where we can say this is truly a direction that has lasting positive effects. This is your choice to make.

CHAPTER 19

Sharing

I s what makes us real human beings, and it is probably the one quality that can make us the most God-like. It is the one action that can help us the most in becoming truly happy and fulfilled.

If I can help you put your arms the concept of sharing, you'll grasp one of the most powerful secrets to be a happy and successful person. The wonderful thing is that it's never too late to start. Rent a copy of Charles Dickens' "A Christmas Carol" for a reminder.

The great minds of spirituality came to know that the preeminent quality of God is sharing. Think about that.

Let's say a miracle happened and you received a check in the mail, and you could fill in the amount. No strings attached whatsoever. So fast forward. You've bought all the houses, boats, planes, clothes, cars, trips, and amazing

ould imagine. You've gotten every single
sh done. So, now what?

re sincerely honest with yourself, you'll find an
ling in the end. If you stopped this obsessive
spe.. ; and decided to help someone, or something with
your money, you will connect in a small way to what the
sharing energy of God feels like.

The amazing aspect of this, is that this act of sharing
does not deplete your money but in fact, encourages even
more money to come your way. This is not my concept
because there are a zillion examples of this in books, movies,
plays, and real life. I'm just here to remind you.

Let's move on to sharing without money attached.

If anyone is looking for the magic pill for a happy and
a fulfilled life, take a pill of sharing. Why is this so? It is so
because the ultimate road to clarity and spiritual happiness
is to reduce the ego whenever possible. It takes us out of
the "me" mentality.

If the sharing is done from an honest and sincere place
without a "me" agenda, reducing the ego is a guarantee.
However, if it is merely the appearance of sharing, it can
be corrupted and the results will be far less satisfying when
personal gains are the motive. So, sharing does come with
some rules; universal laws that even apply with the sharing
of food, wealth, knowledge, and time. Because sharing is
so powerful and so important, to do it right has its cosmic
rules; too much or too little is also a part of it.

Embrace sharing. It comes in all shapes and forms:
money, talent, time, ideas, food (a favorite of mine), words,
knowledge, feelings, etc. As you can see, there really isn't
a shortage. The most important thing is to try and keep
it in the front of your mind.

When I think of my friends of the past whom I have

admired, it all came to the fact that they were givers. Even back then as a kid I was always attracted to other kids who were nice kids. They shared their lunch at times and most had a nice smile on their faces. They seem to be blessed at the early age to know this concept of sharing because they seemed to be the happiest even back then.

One last thing. My son taught me an important lesson about sharing when I pulled out two dollars to give to a homeless person at a stop sign. He said, "Dad, what can he do with two dollars, give him a twenty!" Understand, this was a period of being very lean money-wise. But I took out the twenty because I knew my son was right. Believe me, it hurt. But I did give him the money and he was in shock. He smiled, and his words, "God bless you" still stays with me today. That's what I call a great return on your investment!

1.   Sharing helps us with appreciation.

2.   Look for those difficult areas of sharing.

3.   Look for areas easy to share.

CHAPTER 20

Comfort is the Sure Road to Disaster

It is a hidden psychological suicide pill that will do you in every single time. Now mind you, I'm not talking about living comfortably or having a comfortable living situation. Everyone deserves that. The comfort I'm talking about is more about being too complacent which is an easy place to find ourselves.

Every success, every accomplishment, promotion, etc., what did it ultimately create? After that happy moment of buying that new fancy car, house, TV, suit, dress, comes another voice, a very powerful voice, hmm…how come the excitement is gone? Do I have to buy another suit, house, dress, another promotion, another million dollars to recapture that fleeting thrill? For some people, we all know that is the sad truth. Without exception, we all know those people and how unhappy they are. They make the buy; the thrill is there but leaves as fast as it came. The answer to happiness, to fulfillment, is not that moment because that moment is a cheap feeling of an empty prize.

Instead, it is what it took to acquire that house, car, dress. What it took, the desire you had, the ups and downs, the process of hiring, firing, arguments settlements, negotiations...all those things you have decided that you're saying you're tired of. They are, in fact, the things you never made peace with and found value in them.

I know this can be a big bite to swallow, and you can throw this book away right now, but if you are honest, really honest, think about it. Take a moment, clear your head. Check out for yourself all those defining moments in your life, the anxious moments, the feeling of defeat that led to that feeling of success. If you can relook at and redefine this amazing process, the challenge of it all, instead of feeling anger, offended, ill-treated, and on and on, embrace those moments where you had to dig down deep, and then...smile about them, let them warm your heart, because it is those moments that are remembered. You just need to see them from a positive perspective.

How is this all connected to comfort? The answer is subtle but very profound. Change your perception of your past. Remember, this book is to accelerate you, to help you get excited again, to get you off your you-know-what, because there is something unfinished inside you. The unfinished business that needs to get out. If that's the case, then it will take an effort to get back in the game of life. But on the upside, it may only be a simple misunderstanding of what's keeping you from that brass ring.

Back to chapter 3: The Mind is a Beautiful Thing

and remember, it is a double-edged sword. One side is a prison of bad ideas, bad interpretations, bad, or even evil, inclinations. The fact is that we all have them. Really and honestly, we all have them.

However, on the better side of the sword, is God's gifts. Yes, these do take a little effort. This is why comfort can be our big enemy. But what's most important is to acknowledge that our innate desire to free ourselves is still alive, and we realize we need to open our eyes and resent anything that shackles us to complacency. That's our jail. The difference between me and some of you is that I have found some of the keys that have unlocked those locks.

Because you have paid the price of this book I am obligated to hand over those keys, but you must put the key in the lock of the prison door and turn the key to freedom. I will help show you how you got in jail, what keeps you there, and what you need to get on that road of freedom with proper tools to go past GO, collect $200.00, and rekindle the fire inside.

Back to the title of this chapter: "comfort" and its evil ways. Look, this book may not be for everyone. I have tried to be upfront and direct in this book and my words to those who think they have something left or in the best-case scenario, discover you *do* have something more, another chapter or two, or three, or whatever, inside. For those who have decided life is all but done, and there's nothing left, God bless you. Because the one component required to get the engines going again is the six-letter word called **desire**. Without it, nothing is going to happen even if it falls in your lap. And here is where comfort collides with desire. It's like oil and water...the two cannot coexist. If you have the desire, or if you can conjure it up, you have a chance...a very good chance. Without it, well…it's like getting a brand-new Ferrari with no engine. Get the point? No pedal to the metal! So where do you get this desire? I thought you would never ask because it is a part of an upcoming chapter called, "Passion, Desire and Certainty". You have my permission to skip ahead to it if you wish.

Remember what I was saying about those empty moments of success? The irony of how to keep the desire fired up is going to, perhaps, be a little upsetting. It is contrary to what our society has been pushing…that is being "satisfied". The moment we feel satisfied, desire diminishes. Check it out for yourself. I understand what many of you are probably saying, "You mean, I can't feel good about myself?"

This concept I just plopped on your lap is not an easy thing to swallow. Trust me, I was Mr. Feel Good. But I spent the time thinking about it. Every time I looked for that approval, that satisfaction, something happened, and it wasn't good. There's a saying in the movie business, "What have you done lately?" Trust me it haunts every great filmmaker out there, but it is also what propels them to make the next movie.

Well, maybe it's time to send the message to the world that life, at our age is still a process of learning. And learning from our stage in life is very, very exciting, as we'll discover in the chapter called, "Enjoy New Things, it is a Great High". It is a high because it should lead us to desire more and more life. Those challenging times of the agony of defeat that led to the thrill of the victory are truly where it's at.

CHAPTER 21

Move to
Unconditional Love

"Unconditional Love" is a lesson many seniors have learned through years of living life. They discovered that a policy of "forgive and forget" is the only policy if one expects to find peace of mind and peace of heart. No wonder it is also considered to be one of the very most important spiritual obligations placed upon man by God. But for those who are more stubborn and still wrestling with this I thought I'd brake down some of the spiritual elements required to get you over the hump.

However, getting to this understanding requires some wisdom. But before that, let's start with some simple mistakes we have all made one time or another with a couple of familiar scenarios.

Ladies first, as they say. Ok, your husband forgets to put out the garbage. Are you already feeling your insides getting tight? Are you about to leap out with something ugly to say? If your honest answer is "yes", then just hold on and stop. Take a spiritual breath. It will be the most important breath you can take. Trust me, contrary to some psychologist, this is not a time to express yourself or your feelings. Instead, spiritual wisdom says, restrict your comments and open yourself to "forgive" him right then and there! I don't care how you find that place of forgiveness inside yourself but find it even if you must fight to find it. Love him for all the other times he did it right.

I know years of bad habits can take time to correct. Besides, no one is perfect, not you, me or him (whomever that may be). That is why God's system allows for saying, "sorry". Let's leave it at that.

Now you guys. You come home tired from all those outside challenges relieved to shut the door behind you. Then off in the background your wife belts out that she forgot to tell you about a dinner engagement. Of course, it's with your least favorite couple you've been cursed with for the last thirty years. Sound familiar?

Here's where you are faced with your choices; you can be reactive and go down the same old path by voicing the same old words of anger or disappointment or... choice two, take a pause. Allow yourself to feel your negative energy inside. And here is where the miracle occurs, and work is required. Replace those negative feelings with a loving or positive thought, tough as it may be. The more you allow for something positive to fill that space the more you will experience "unconditional love". It is an awesome life process to experience you can't help but embrace. And by the way, it will even work with your bothersome neighbor.

To even brake it down even further, think of your good angel or bad angel.

When we send someone unconditional love we get a piece of the pie as well, so to speak. By connecting to our heart and allowing our self to send them love, you feel it as well. Why do you receive unconditional love? Because you are opening your heart which is tapping into God's energy. God's energy is mainly a sharing energy, so we are guaranteed to receive the benefits when we tap into it.

The main component that blocks our effort to embrace "unconditional love" is our own ego. I know I keep talking about the ego, but the topic naturally comes up a lot in this arena. If you can conjure up the feelings of someone who has disappointed you and call up those ugly feelings of betrayal, disappointment, etc., etc., it all comes from the ego and takes on the persona called the "victim". You can now see how the dark side is so slick and slippery. The answer? First, we must acknowledge that no one is a victim. God gave every single human being the tools to succeed. That is probably the biggest pill many people find the hardest to swallow but the soonest you acknowledge that, the sooner you can get to work and reap the benefits of spiritual work.

Finding happiness through spirituality is never about the other person. It's about your own internal condition and your ability to transform your negative traits into proactive, positive traits like finding "unconditional love". You'll see it comes from your own heart, your own eyes, ears, your own desire for peace and happiness. Not only does it cost you nothing, but the added prize is that it hands back a heart that is happy and at peace.

Now don't think I have not struggled with this concept myself. The fact of it is that I still do. No one is perfect and yes, it is an ongoing process that gets challenged each time a new rude, and angry person comes my way.

I have learned to use my heart as my own "truth meter". I think of those negative people out there (and there are no shortage of jerks) and feel how those bad feelings affect me and my heart. Not good, right? So, do I want to keep those bad feelings? Heck no!

Instead, I want to rid myself of those bad feelings every time I think about those people because sending them more negative energy will never help. The old spiritual adage says, "you can't fight darkness with darkness". So, the simple solution is to send them "Light" or positive energy. And if it is still too difficult for me to do it, I ask God to send it.

And in case you're wondering, I learned that another of God's gifts are to take care of those evil and nasty people for you. Even though it may not appear that way, trust me, God has his ways.

Though you may say, "look at them, they are rich, and they live in a big beautiful house." But if you look closer, you'll see the cracks where pain and suffering are lurking in their life. It could be drug or alcohol addiction within family members, or a very unhealthy marriage. But one thing I promise, they are far from happy. I have seen this too many times myself throughout the years. I'm not saying to gloat in this but do not take on God's responsibility.

If someone did you wrong, well, as the saying goes "What goes around comes around". I absolutely promise. You may not get the satisfaction of knowing it, but it is a universal law. What I'm saying is, leave God's work to God. We're not qualified except if you're a mafia kind of guy, then this book is probably not for you.

Hand over that responsibility to the higher power,

then you have the freedom to "forgive" knowing there's a better entity for the job, and truly let it go. Lighten your load. Feel the tightness leave your chest. It's a great feeling...because it's a feeling of "freedom". Letting go and forgiveness go hand and hand. Remember my father's saying, "He who travels lightest, travels fastest".

If we want to put smiles where frowns are, then forgiveness and letting go are a must. And now what's left is the ultimate prize I promised earlier. Fill that void where negativity claimed its home and put a loving feeling to take its place and be a proud bearer of "Unconditional love" and a true beacon of God's Light.

CHAPTER 22

Look for the Newness in Things

It's a great high and a concept that really captivates me. It is a lot like many things we do in life that are taken for granted.

The new car, the new love, the new dog, the new day, the new show, the new movie, the new friend, the new shoes, the new idea, the new phone, the new moon, and on and on and on. It's exhilarating. Let's leave this extensive list behind for a moment and investigate why the heck "newness" is even a part of our human experience.

The first thing I think of is that it feels so good. It has a built-in adrenaline rush…and who doesn't like that!

In God's infinite wisdom, he gave us tools to succeed in life. Newness is one of them. It can only be a tool if we look at it as such. So, if you can follow me and embrace newness as a tool then we can take full use of this awesome experience.

Step one. Remember that newness is a very pleasant feeling. Though it may appear to be a fleeting feeling, it does have a unique quality to be retrieved, recalled if you may.

Let's look at *personal relationships*. Think about it. this tool is one of the most important concepts in personal relationships that keep things fresh and evolving. When things seem boring, God is tapping you on the shoulder to tell you to relook at things. It is His way of reminding you to get off your butt-zone and discover a fresh, more fulfilling perception about your friend, lover, or family member. Until you arrive at a truth that involves giving more to the other person, you'll need to keep looking.

The same concept applies to personal situations such as work, non-work, too much money, not enough money. Boredom is the red-flag nudge given to you that says, "Hey, I'm not moving until you do something 'new'." What an amazing system!

Let's look at love—new, fresh love. There may not be any more powerful feeling as love and when it enters your life everything changes.

A new love is impenetrable. No matter what anyone may say in opposition, their voice will fall on deaf ears because there is no room for negative thoughts or comments from anyone: your mother, brother, sister, father, or friend. They will turn instantly into "the enemy".

The problem occurs when the newness wears off, because then the dark side enters. Look at it as the party pooper. You see, the dark side of us does not want us to be happy. Its job is at stake. So, they attack all those beautiful observations fiercely chipping away until all the goodness, the happiness, gets turned into crap. The antidote? Reconnect to those first new impressions where that new and powerful love was created. Connecting you in the first place. Dismiss those negative voices as voices that don't belong in your mind.

I think the same occurs with other examples of the newness experience. Putting aside the "new Ferrari" fantasy, which will lose its glitter the first time you bring it for a tune-up and you get the bill, let's take a better route.

Let me throw out something different, something that delivers a lifetime of fulfillment.

Remember, many years ago the words my father said, "He who travels lightest, travels fastest". That has stayed with me a lifetime. The moment those words came out of his mouth for the first time, it hit me like a lightning bolt. I somehow knew those words would serve me for a lifetime. They were words I had never heard before but strangely it struck to my core and became an everlasting beacon of wisdom. It has never lost its luster and still retains its quality as if I just heard those words a moment ago.

The more I think about this topic of newness, the more mind-boggling it becomes. I have learned that each day is new and unique.

So, for me, each morning I pray to improve things from the prior day. It's sort of the philosophy of "what have I done for you lately" to myself. It helps in clearing the slate and capturing the new day with all its glitter.

Resting on one's laurels only sets us up for disappointment. I found that out with my son. There are times when I expected him to appreciate me for all the wonderful things I have done as his father. The truth is, he would begrudgingly say, "Sure, Dad I appreciate all those things," but deep down inside, I know he's saying, "Okay, enough Dad, stop with this self-adulation stuff." Well, you know…it's true.

Maybe this is the key to why God made newness so special. What does holding on to those past actions do for me anyway? In truth, it's only more food for the ego.

The lesson is…opts for a clean slate. Each day can be so filled with unlimited "new" ideas, actions. I know it sounds robust, but it isn't.

Let this feeling of newness invigorate you every day. Just allow it. It's free of charge, and you don't need a doctor's prescription.

The other benefit of newness is that it reminds us that God has given this gift to forgive ourselves and move freely to doing things better. With each morning I wake up to a new day reminding myself that today I have that ability to do a better job than yesterday.

If we take that consciousness seriously, each day can be unique, and we will throw boredom out the window. If we truly try to improve on each and every new day we have on this planet, life as we know it becomes fresh, and we are forced to be "engaged". We become attached to the day based on a commitment to do better in every way we can.

I promise that no matter what we have left to give, it will become stronger and produce a solid source of discovery and real fulfillment that's far better than that new pair of shoes.

Be aware of the excitement of a new month because it brings new energy:

1. How you can be new in conversation, go through your comfort zone.

2.   Try new things and see how people respond.

3.   You can be the creator of newness in a positive way.

4.   Newness helps you from being so predictable.

5.   The new you.

CHAPTER 23

Taking the "First Step"

Conjures up for me the idea of the universe and everything there is to know about it. Can you imagine what the consciousness of God must have been when he made the first step to create man? Chilling!

I just wanted to embrace this concept to set the stage of how important making the first step really is. This is not to scare you but to encourage you.

Taking the first step for me has always been associated with doing something important, something maybe even life-changing. I can't ever remember when taking that first step led me down the wrong path of being reckless. How's that? Because there is a practical side to this that kept me from jumping off the cliff with an attached bungee cord.

What I prefer doing is to go through a checklist to kind of get me looking at my intentions. The questions I ask myself are: Why am I even doing this? Will it be helpful for people or am I doing this new adventure for my ego? Secondly, is it reasonable? Does it kind of make sense? Am I going to teach math at NASA? No, I hope not! But is it reasonable to think of teaching math for third graders? "Yes, I can do that!" And there you go…I became a substitute teacher.

It did require a big first step, but I put together a bit of a game plan, which included visiting other classrooms to kind of get the lay of the land and check into the actual need for substitute teachers. In short, I did some homework and prepared. I let the energy of excitement carry me through this process.

You'll discover when you embrace this concept that it has built-in adrenaline. Whether it is a physical step towards some kind of medical recovery or making a phone call, it conjures up a ball of energy that includes some fear and excitement rolled into one. I wonder what God was feeling when he took His first step and decided to create the universe. Holy tamale!

This sort of opens the proverbial can of worms, wouldn't you say?

Another important thing I found out about taking that first step is to decide whether it's being done from a reactive place or a more proactive place. The meaning being: are you taking this first step out of anger, resentment, jealousy, payback, or some other negative emotion? If that's the case trust me, drop it like a hot potato! Your actions will bite you…HARD.

Just for the fun of it, let's just list some of these "first step" ideas or actions.

Write your first step ideas here:

1.

2.

3.

4.

5.

CHAPTER 24

Money

I f you think I'm going to give you a great stock tip, think again!

Money is an awesome topic. It fed your family, got your car, put a roof over your head, clothes on your back, got your kids through school. That's the first tier.

Second tier: it sent you and family on vacation, bought nice clothes for your wife, and maybe some fancy jewelry, nice car, amazing house. Most of us had to go through the process and as years pass, your "money surplus" builds and builds till you get that smile either on your face, or a smile inside your mind, and definitely in your pocket.

The way I look at money these days has grossly changed. I went from being a multi-millionaire most of my life to living off social security. Believe me, it is a big gap. Make no mistake, being poor has its built-in pressures; it's burdensome. But believe it or not, it has huge benefits. I know there are those in the back row about to throw up! But hold that.

Being poor is worrisome, and that actually is where the benefits hide.

These are the things I learned:

1. Budgeting.
2. Budgeting and detailing expenses.
3. Learn to curtail your wasteful spending.
4. Better for the ecology.
5. Better for the economy by lowering excessive debt.
6. Gives us a more practical perspective.
7. Teaches our kids more restraint.
8. Teaches us what is really of value.
9. Better understanding of charity.
10. Money is a pure energy/can be positive or negative.
11. Intent.
12. What is security?
13. What is money greed?

Having no money did not turn me against money. Instead, it taught me to take a serious look at what makes the world work on many levels. If I accept this as something God also put into our minds, then it certainly should not be disregarded.

This chapter is purely for you to take another look at money without going through what I did. To do that, is it important to connect to the emotional triggers that money conjures up. I am sure there are many because money is connected to almost everything. What I hope we can agree on is that money is basically a spiritual tool and it should be treated as such.

One of the most basic spiritual principles about money is to give a minimum of 10% of your earnings to charity. This maybe a difficult pill for some to swallow but for those who already know of its deep benefits, I bet not one of you will say it didn't help create more wealth because it is a universal and spiritual law. Aside from the monetary benefits, it will truly make you feel happy if it's given in a real sincere way.

Because this subject can be super complex, I have kept it short. But let me throw out some concepts instead☺.

1. Question purchases as to how much they really benefit you. For me it used to be "art" because I, as well as those around me, enjoyed it daily.

2. Lending money always seems to be a sore point for most because we all know people rarely repay. What I have learned is that the moment you give out the money, let it go, and if possible, with a smile.

3. Money is not Love. Love is love. Unconditional giving is love.

4. Finally, money is a complex tool God created and allowed you to manage. Check with Him to see how well you're doing.

CHAPTER 25

Passion, Desire, and Certainty

Are probably the three most important qualities needed for a human being to be happy, truly successful, and live to fulfillment.

Passion, desire, and certainty are all there for the taking and they're free. You just have to find the switch inside of you that connects to them and flip it.

Become familiar with these most powerful emotions even if they are from the past. The process to reconnect to passion, desire, and certainty is invigorating. It's medicine. Whether it's a memory of the past, or something new, it doesn't matter. The spiritual fact is that they are true emotions that are fuel for the soul.

According to some experts, our energy is endless,

and it is only a matter of removing the mental blocks and connecting to God's tools that unleashes its power. Personally, I have found that to be true. If it weren't, I couldn't write this book, be a good father, teacher, or friend.

The more you absolutely connect to these words, the more benefits you'll receive. This is not theory; this is a proven fact. I know the negative voices inside will argue with all their might, but it is just a mental argument from the dark side; don't give in to it. I'm not asking you to run a marathon or do things beyond your physical abilities. Passion, desire, and certainty are concepts that have no physical limits in your mind. They are amazing tools. So, let's look at them:

For me, passion is my fuel. It is amazing how this energy force, which seems to be unique to us humans, has played such a prominent role in all our lives, and in the development of humanity. It's a driver; it's a gift. At some point in our lives, haven't we all connected with some sort of passion? Something that drove us to further heights? Isn't passion the basis for most of our joy?

It is an accelerator that tingles the body, puts smiles on our faces, and produces energy within us that people pick up on just by looking at us. It is truly God-given. Of course, it is a fickle force as well. It can leave us. It can die. But it can be revived too! Because this book is spiritual in nature, I will speak to you in spiritual terms that are easily comprehended.

Finding your passion can be like going fishing. It takes desire to catch the fish, confidence that there's even fish out there, and thirdly, certainty. Sometimes, to reconnect to passion, desire needs to be reawakened. Passion is very powerful, and we don't need to be afraid. It is a life giver, a life saver.

Of course, we now know within the confines of a spiritual and pursuable life that everything happens for a reason. That means every emotion as well. God equipped us with a toolbox filled with everything imaginable. Why? Because He loves us that much.

I'm saying this to remind you that desire, passion, and certainty are blessed tools He wants us to use, and, like I said, they are free for the taking. So, when it comes into our lives, treat it with respect.

1. Divine inspiration.

2. Is there science?

3. Everyone has it.

4. How to build on it.

5. How to create a relationship with it.

6. A great creative tool.

7. It's there all the time; remember it and it appears.

8. It has many faces.

9. Desire is my other fuel.

10. Certainty is what really takes work. It's power to create miracles.

11. Certainty is knowing that what whatever happens, there is a reason for it.

CHAPTER 26

Hundreds of Millions of People Pray Every Day

I assume that every one of you have prayed at least once in your life. But has anyone ever taken the time to figure out how it really works?

I was surprised when I heard the more acknowledged account of Moses, and what really happened at the splitting of the Red Sea. Pharaoh and his troops were quickly catching up to the Israelites, ready to slaughter them all as they were backed up to the sea with nowhere to go. Now, if there was a time to pray, that was the time.

Here is why we pray... We think it's when life appears overwhelming and we believe we've run out of answers. Well, as the story of Moses points out, when God was asked to step in and save the Israelites from an eminent massacre, God's surprise answer was, "Why ask me, you have the power to do it yourself." Wow, what an answer!

It is said that within each one of us we have been given the DNA from God. The problem, of course, is that we forget. We forget how awesome and powerful we as human beings are. So, when I pray, I ask to be reminded of my DNA, so I can ask the right questions and to keep me as close to Him in my consciousness as possible. Because without God, I am lost. So, keeping him close should be our most important prayer and when we put this all together with "certainty", something happens that becomes the most powerful example of the existence of God Himself, and that is "miracles".

MIRACLES

Why do we all love miracles? Movies, books, and songs have used miracles as a theme, plot line, or event. It is the best kind of drama that works every single time, without fail, and are a solid a reason to believe in God as anything. But what is central to most, if not all this drama? The answer is…hopelessness. It is the feeling that all is lost with no help in sight. The end of the road, so to speak. We know the Egyptians are coming and have no possibility of escape…but we do, says God. They're called one of his greatest of gifts: miracles.

But there is a secret to miracles and how to create more miracles in your life. Typically, when a miracle occurs in your life, you feel relieved and even thankful. The crisis is over, and we can move on. But that is where we fall short. The real secret most people fail to acknowledge is the amazing act of the miracle itself. If we shift our focus to how mind boggling a miracle is, then we get to appreciate God's power. We can see the difference between a reality of having God's influence in our daily lives or not. The more we see how unique and amazing God's work is through his miracles, the more miracles come your way. The reason is because of our friend, "certainty". It adds fuel to the fire.

Both my kids were adopted. It was during that adoption that I truly found God, and it too was revealed through a miracle. Here is the story…

It was a very cold, wintery morning as my wife and I arrived in Almaty, Kazakhstan. We had gone through too many hours of non-sleep airplane rides from California, arriving in this third world country that 99 percent of Americans never even heard of. I thought for sure I was in the middle of some black and white movie of the fifties, as the ugly American center-staged in some bizarre adventure. Thank God, I am a seasoned traveler and trusted in my New York savviness to maneuver me through this new and strange setting as we arrived in the airport, reminiscent of the airport in the movie "Casablanca".

After finally getting up from our seats I dared not make eye contact with my wife for fear she would see a crack in my persona of confidence. This persona was all I had left that kept me intact.

Coming down the steps of this out-of-date Russian plane I nervously scanned the crowd hoping to catch the eye of a person looking for two very out-of-place Americans. Believe me, my heart was pounding. And whatever that magnetic energy we humans possess to connect to that searching counterpart, it zoomed in on this attractive woman with a very warm and welcoming smile.

"Are you Mr. and Mrs. Horowitz?"

Those words instantly deflated my anxiety. I responded

with a confident, "Yes." To myself I said, "Thank you, God!"

But of course, life can never be so easy because in her marginal English, she said, "We'll check into the hotel tonight and catch another plane tomorrow to the orphanage." Yes, another flight, another day of travel. And so, it went.

The following morning, we boarded a Russian 1950's military prop plane. I can't say it was converted for commercial use; it was just used for commercial use. The metal seats attested to its origin. Anyway, off we went for a memorable three-hour flight thinking all along we'd probably have to take this very plane again on the way back!

It was still early that cold November morning. The car pulled through the heavy wrought iron gates to what looked like an old brick factory building of the early sixties vintage in New York's lower East Side. The anticipation was unimaginable. Ahead, in that old building, on an ice-cold morning with smoke steaming out of various pipes, was housed my new family.

The three of us were quickly ushered through a door into narrow hallways filled with the scurry of women carrying anything from towels to clothes, to who knows what. Finally, we all arrived at the office of the director of the orphanage.

Out stepped this well-dressed woman in her late forties to early fifties with a firm but nice, welcoming smile. Barely having time to catch my breath, our interpreter said that the director was happy to see us arriving safely, but there was no time to waste. We needed to claim our daughter and then pick out our son. "What, seriously. Pick out our son?", I said.

"First let's see your daughter who's upstairs in the

nursery," responded the interpreter. So, without hesitation, off we went.

As a side note, our daughter, Skye was spoken for months in advance and was eight months old. We'd wanted a boy as well, but they said back at our adoption center in New York that there were plenty of boys of suitable age to choose from. They said that can be decided on when we got there. Of course, the key wordings were, "after a while".

Upstairs, we entered the nursery where our new baby was crying in her crib. A nurse hovered over her with a very worried look. They told us she had been throwing up the formula they gave her and was dehydrating. My anxiety levels skyrocketed. But my wife, Marsha, who seemed knowledgeable about this kind of thing, calmly asked if they could get goats milk. They nodded, yes. Hey, of course, we were in Kazakhstan where goats roamed the streets! It seemed like it took only moments before the goat's milk was in hand, and Skye was happily sucking it up with no trouble. At this point, Marsha took full charge of our new baby girl. Welcome to instant fatherhood!

Marsha, with the baby in her arms, myself, our interpreter, and a nurse, all scuttled downstairs as if time was of the essence. We were greeted by the director again, who stood in front of the large open room filled with little boys and a firm smile. The director spoke in Russian to our interpreter and what came out will forever be branded in my memory. Mr. Horowitz? "Time to pick out your son."

My face went flushed as I looked over to my wife holding tightly onto Skye. "Now?" I eked out. "Yes," the director said in perfect English. "That's how we do it here." It's was as defining a moment as any man can ever have.

Holding on to her words, shook me to my core. How was I going to pick out a small child in ten minutes' time, and say, "Hey you. You are now my son till death do us part!"

I needed a moment...by myself.

Without saying a word, they watched as I went off and turned the corner of the hallway. Halfway down I stopped and stood alone in my silence, terrified.

This was truly a dream, a moment out of a classic film, or at best some kind of mistake. My logical mind couldn't grasp how bizarre this all was. How could I possibly make such a decision that would affect my life, his life, Marsha's life, just like that?! It was absurd, and totally crazy!

Finding God can be shocking. Because it was at that moment and totally out of character, I said to myself, "God, please help me, please show me a sign!" Whether I just took those words from a book I once read, or from somewhere else, I don't know. But those were the words that came to me. And with a false sense of confidence, I walked back with everyone's eyes fixed on me. I said, "I think I'm ready."

Trust me, I couldn't make this up. It really happened.

So, now coming slowly toward us, three little boys all around 3-4 years of age. They walked cautiously, almost arm in arm, shy and deathly quiet. Intently, I looked for a sign, but nothing happened... Nothing but blank eyes and forlorn faces.

A second group of three boys of the same ages walked up to us, staring with their deep, dark eyes and little to no expression. I turned toward my wife with nothing more than an anxious look. How could this be real? The boys were asked to turn around and go back. The feelings I felt rejecting these kids could never be expressed in words. It may have well been my lowest moment in my life. Sadness falls way too short as a word.

A third set of boys came toward us, with one boy's arm

in a sling. From the corner of my eye, I saw Marsha wiping a tear or two as she held our new baby girl very close and secure to her chest.

And, just as I turned back to those boys, something happened…

This one child looked straight into my eyes and smiled. It was so broad and brightly lit up it made me freeze as if time itself had stopped. He didn't stop smiling. His bright eyes were so alive, so full of happiness, it was as if God Himself was being revealed through him. To this day I am convinced He was.

I was totally transfixed. I just couldn't stop looking. Suddenly, Marsha nudged me and as if to awaken me from a dream. I turned to her and said, "He's our boy; he's the one."

That was my miracle. It was also the moment when I truly found God, and my amazing son, Anton. Thank you, God!

Since then I have learned that miracles occur in all shapes and sizes. In fact, I have grown to understand that every second we are alive is a miracle. Though less dramatic, the miracle of Skye coming into our lives is as remarkable and as profound as Anton's story.

She is perfect in every way. Loving, kind, a gifted artist, an amazing singer, and someone who loves me and her brother unconditionally, not to mention Marsha, her mom. The most critical point here is to have the ability and the awareness to see these all with immense appreciation. Without appreciation, miracles seem to vanish before our very eyes. These extraordinary gifts become mere events with no sparkle or knowledge as being gifts of any kind.

The truth of the matter: other kinds of miracles occur in our lives all the time. The only thing is, we may not be aware of them. They are called, "the unseen or unknown miracles".

Of course, we have all heard stories about people missing planes only to find out that the plane they missed crashed. They didn't ask for the miracle. They didn't even want to be the cause of those miracles, because of those who were less fortunate. But nonetheless, they are bona fide miracles, and their meanings can be well hid by God, Himself.

In short, it is all about opening our eyes to life itself. The simple to the complex. Miracles are all around us; it is just a simple choice to see it that way.

CHAPTER 27

Fear

Writing this chapter proved to be more complicated than I anticipated. The fact of the matter, "fear", I discovered, has many faces. My discovery was that fear is one of the most important and required emotions/instincts all living beings must have.

Case in point.

Once I spent a lot of time sailing. It can be a dangerous endeavor, especially when racing. There were all kinds of weather conditions, people bumping into each other, choppy waves, big intimidating waves, sails going up and down sideways, you name it. You might say it was coordinated chaos. But because there was always some sort of danger lurking, there had to be some steadfast rules.

Falling overboard was, of course, one of those most feared dangers. My rule for that danger was straightforward: "Don't fall overboard!"

How this relates to fear is simple yet intriguing to me. In our decision-making process, especially in a potentially dangerous situation, fear can be our best ally; it brings out our common sense. "Stay out of harm's way, if possible!" Okay, are we very clear about that? Allowing your fear factor to work for you can be life-saving. So, you see, even fear can be positive if correctly used.

Another case in point: don't open a cage when a lion is in it! Sounds silly, doesn't it? However, haven't we heard of bizarre stories where some idiot does just that? This is where it gets a little interesting. Here the ego enters and convinces us that, "Hey buddy, haven't you heard you must confront your fears? So, let's open that cage!" Right then, I believe God would say, "Gee, I'm sorry but at this point, you're on your own."

The idea I hope to get across is that like all other emotions and feelings, fear is just another tool given to us by God, but we need to learn how to use it.

This may be an exaggerated example, and most of us would never turn that key in the lock, but we have all allowed our egos to make bad decisions when it teams up with fear.

Driving is one of those situations that come immediately to mind. This, to me is a perfect example of where a "sense of fear" can keep you alive. But on the other hand, it can also become deadly if you allow your ego to intervene and show you how fast your new Mercedes can go when your better judgment says, "No!" So, you see here again, fear is double edged.

Can you now see more clearly how sneaky the ego can

get? Left alone, your fear of opening that cage and testing the speed of that car is a blessing and should be greatly appreciated.

Let's talk about the different faces of fear: The Good, the Bad, and the Ugly, and how they are so much different.

At times, I think of fear as having actual human qualities in of itself. It's like looking at a human being with many disguises. What I mean is that fear can be gentle, it can be good, just like we've seen, and it can be very nasty. When it gets nasty and very bad, fear is one of the most terrifying feelings or emotions humans can have. How can we tame the beast, when it becomes the beast?

Let's start off with a twist by saying how much we even appreciate Mr. Bad and Ugly Fear! That's right. Mr. Bad and Ugly Fear (my new name for him) can be bad to the bone. He has many disguises, and creeps in like a well-trained marine. It almost takes an act of God to escape his grip. So, why did I start off by embracing this monster?

The simple answer first. We are talking about the physiological fear, the "fake" fear, if you will. It's the most feared-fear because it's not even real! How do I know? I know because I have pulled the veil off its face more times than I can remember!

In fact, I think God created this monster to give us humans some sort of entertainment tool to be used in novels, T.V. shows, movies, and for older brothers and sisters, to harass their younger brothers and sisters! Okay... So, who thinks I'm kidding, raise your hand? Okay, now put them down now.

The genuine answer is...

I believe God gave us this Mr. Bad Fear, so we can better find God Himself!

Let's look at the end game.

I mean, when we are terrified beyond belief, what happens? We become disabled, frozen to the core. Women scream, men freeze. All is lost.

Some will look for "Ghostbusters" but that's the wrong answer. That's the problem with Hollywood. What is the right answer? The right answer *is*…God!

Of course, it's God!

Because God is truly the only answer where true peace and safety exists. But if you are looking for an exception to the golden rule, then look in the mirror. There lies the one and only one caveat. It's also ourselves!

Let's all take a deep breath and let this settle in.

God gave us His DNA, which says a lot. Our problem is that we mostly forget that. But, if we are at the top of our spiritual game, and we can apply this awareness, manmade miracles will happen! The splitting of the Red Sea is a case in point.

So, why all this "stuff", all this drama? I think God added this powerful Mr. Bad Ugly Fear as a "wake-up" shock therapy, a kind of last resort element to bring people back to Him or the Him inside of us. So, if that's the case, then we must thank God with as much appreciation we can muster up. I am sure that some of you have experienced this "end of the road" fear that led you to God and brought you back to your senses.

As a recap to this very difficult chapter, let me summarize a few things: The first is that fear and its many different faces are "tools". Just like any other tool, we need to learn how to use it and recognize it as such. This tool called fear has its own intrinsic complexities. But the one secret, the one truth I will leave with you, is that "Fear is a tool designed to lead you straight to God!"

CHAPTER 28

Smiling

I am proud to say that Anton had his bar mitzvah last year. As part of his process he needed to say a few words. He asked me if it was okay to talk about smiling. He said he had written something about smiling and wondered if it would be appropriate to talk about it now. I said, of course. So, I would like to share his words about smiling, by Anton Horowitz, and that will be all I'll say about the subject. ☺

Laughing is music, laughing is light and easygoing, laughter is making someone's day that much brighter, laughter is positive, and laughter is energy. Laughter is like a violin; it makes a beautiful sound. A beautiful image of positivity. Laughter has the power to heal. Laughter can stop time and aging by connecting to your soul. Someone was one time complaining to me and then I laughed at something just randomly. Then the whole situation lightened up. There is a reason that I laugh at these serious situations. That's because I needed to lighten up, and my soul was telling me, "It's time to not feel so bummed out." One laugh can fix depression. Or one smile. It takes more muscles to frown or feel bad than to smile or laugh. It's a proven fact. There is a reason for this, I believe. We need to laugh more. There can be no mistake about laughing or smiling. It helps the sick and can help anyone any day. Happiness is fulfillment. When I truly get what my soul needs, I feel better because of that.

One situation for me is when I thought I needed those nice Nike shoes, but in reality, any shoes would have worked and really have fulfilled that longing in my heart. So, I ended up getting them for track and field. The first couple days I was excited and felt blessed. Then after about a week I felt played. Played by my emotions. I thought "Wow! I really wanted these, what happened?" The things I thought I needed were disguised as wants and I got sucked down into a sinking abyss a level more. The thing I needed to realize was the thought of appreciation. But the good news is there is a time when I had to make a choice. My soul said, "Think about it. Will this really help improve and fulfill your life?" Happiness and good vibes helped me find and understand that those unfulfilling thoughts were poisoning my life. All you have to do is recognize it.

Thank you,

Anton Horowitz

Skye

CHAPTER 29

Death

That lurking creature that, at one time, was a subject of a faraway idea now comes close to home. How bizarre is it to confront death, what many would call the final stage on this planet? I'm here to say otherwise.

As you know, I have followed the spiritual path here on earth. Why? What's the truthful answer? The short answer is it has proven to be 100 percent correct...no exceptions.

If I look to the spiritual world for my "life" answers, then it would stand to reason to look to them as well for their "death" answers. And here is what they say.

Death is an illusion. Even from a scientific perspective, things don't really die, they just transform to become something else. Even modern-day physics backs me up.

That's the physical. So, what about the other part—the soul we speak so much about? There it gets interesting.

The soul we know is not physical. This is strictly from the world of spirituality but think about it. Aside from any Hollywood version, the soul is our inner voice. It is a true voice that mysteriously guides us down the correct path of life. From where does that voice originate? Is it an actual energy force of some great intelligence? If so let's jump back to science. And science says, "Energy never dies, it just transforms."

I'm not the brightest guy on the block but if energy never dies, then what about our soul, which is much of who we are?

What can possibly happen to the soul, and where could it go, especially if you include the existence of God? My conclusion is that it must go somewhere. Some say Hell and others say Heaven. I've never heard anyone say it goes nowhere.

There are too many documented stories of people who became clinically dead, came alive again and remembered their experience. How many ghost stories have been recorded throughout history? Think how bizarre it would be if death were final. Would religion or spirituality even exist? Sorry, but that just would not make sense, especially when I include how perfectly spirituality works here on earth when we are alive. How can death not be part of the process? How would it work if death were not even part of life, but something separate? Nothing I have heard says that would be true. So now what? This leads me to accept that death is another form of life. This is my belief.

I further believe that life is a preparation for death, and death is a preparation for life. To broaden it further, even the spiritual community has its guidelines. Do good on

Earth, and your death experience is good as in Heaven. Have a bad life experience, and your death experience is bad as in Hell. Makes sense.

As we get older, somehow nature, or God, softens the idea of death. Personally, I don't really fear it. However, twenty years ago, that was a different story. It seems that God has miraculously entered our brain and even taken away that fear.

So, if I was to define death, I would say it is another form, or formless, expression of life, and vice versa.

How about the practical side of death? Yes, I believe there is one. I believe that it is important to leave clean, meaning to complete as much of your business while you're alive. Leaving your garbage here on earth for others to clean up is not cool. Complete as many of your projects on your to-do list as you can. Make a thorough list; you can always add to it. I personally think it adds possible years to your life.

One more point I would like to make is the value of memories. This is something I think of a lot because I often I think of the past. Let's focus on creating as many fond memories as possible. I believe it will keep a part of us here on earth, happy and without any effort.

CHAPTER 30

The Light (force)

The "Light". What the heck is that!? I'm sure there are a few out there saying the same thing." What?!"

Well, the answer to that question is by far the most important truth I offer. The reason being is that the Light is the energy force of God. It is everything, everything, everything. It doesn't get simpler than that...kind of.

When I think of this idea, concept, or truth, it can get overpowering. How can it be so simple, so easy? The simple answer is that it is that simple. The more difficult part is to believe that in your heart.

When I have difficult issues in life ranging from my car to my children, friends, enemies, or anything at all, I look to the Light for help. I wish I could say it is always my first instinct, but honestly, it's not always so. You see, we are all a work in progress.

If I'm not connected, typically at first, I try and figure it out intellectually. That is rationally using my intellect... ego. I don't know about you but when I do this the result never really works. Why? It's because our mind alone gets clouded with all kind of ego stuff: fear, perception, etc.

However, when I just focus on the Light and direct its energy to the issue, I know it is void of that ego stuff, allowing a true solution to eventually unfold.

If there is anything in my book I pray you understand and take into your heart, it's this truth about the Light. It is kind of a true secret of life. It is also why I've left it for the last chapter. I want this to stick. I want you to test, to challenge, to open up to its ultimate and endless power and test the results.

The astonishing thing about the Light is that it is always there for the taking. But like the simple light switch at home, you must take the initiative and flip the switch. You must consciously activate it by acknowledging the Light is God's energy, there to help you. Why is it so important to call it the Light? Let me explain.

When one thinks of God, it is impossible to truly understand the word "God" or truly comprehend it. It's impossible. Each person can take a shot at it but let's face it, it's been tried and, without fail, they've come up short.

However, when one considers the energy of God, we don't have to define it conclusively because energy has its own built-in limitless borders and it's easier to consider. That is why when we talk about the Light as an energy force it is something easier to comprehend. But most important is that the Light is with you everywhere, anytime. No exceptions: 24/7.

Even mainstream society has adopted this concept of the Light without consciously knowing it. What do you think Luke Skywalker is thinking of, or meditating on, when he focuses on the "Force"? Wink, wink. Yes, it's the Light. So, now, for those who are shocked about this revelation, take a breath and exhale. Yes, Luke, the Light is with you; use it. Remember we *are* the Star Wars generation.

Instead of, "Let the Light be with you!" know that "The Light is *always* with you." Just flip the switch and ask for help!

Now, put a smile on your face and put the *pedal to the medal.*

Amen.

Acknowledgments

Anton, my son who is now 16 and Skye, my daughter who is now 13 are who I live for. Having them involved in this book both in content and other input made this experience worth its weight in gold.

They have surprised me in so many positive ways both in their abilities and willingness to contribute. Thank you both from the most blessed father of them all.

Next, I must thank you, Angela Townsend, a great writer and friend who helped me too often to mention, through this arduous process of getting a book to market, especially for a first-time author. Her guidance and advice and referrals made this process a process of friendship I so greatly appreciate.

Thank you, Cindy Davis, my editor, who thank God, did not grade my high school papers and taught me how much I don't know about grammar.

And of course, Grady my designer and illustrator of my amazing book cover. Than you for your patience and talent.

And finally, the lovely Toni Kerr who did a perfect job formatting the interior of my book. Toni, thank you for being such a wonderful and easy person to speak to and being a part of the team.

70 YEARS OF HIGHWAY ROADS

SANFORD J. HOROWITZ

Author, 2015-Present
Whitefish, Montana
Born In Brooklyn, New York

Great Neck North High School
Football, Track, Wrestling
Key Club

Union College B.a.
History/Economic Major
Drama Minor

The US Army 1967-69
Served in the Intelligence Corp
Heidleberg, Germany

**Worked And Lived In New York City
1969-1970**

**Management Assistant
1970-1972 Supervised Construction
and Co Designed**
"Eagles Nest", Residential Home,
Port Antonio, Jamaica, W.I.

Port Antonio Sand and Gravel, Ltd.
President 1970-71

Sailor/Racer/Owner of Classic Sailing Boats
Knickerbocker Yacht Club, Port Washington, New York
California Yacht Club
Marina Del Rey, Ca.
Blue Jays, Lightning, 505, Kickerbocker One Design,
California PC's, Star Boats
Kirawan

Newport-Bermuda Race
2000

**Vice President of Filmmakers
International Releasing Corp.**
Hollywood, California
Co Produced;
California Country
The Clones
Woman In The Rain

**Distributor
VP of Distribution
David Carradine Productions:**
A Country Mile
You And Me
Master's Degree in Cinema
Columbia College,
Hollywood, Ca.
1972-1982
Citicorp Credit Officer
Factoring Division
Los Angeles, Ca.
Players Theatre,
Burbank, Californis

Owner/Artistic Director/Producer/Director

King Of The City
Associate Producer/2Nd Unit Director

Script Writer
The Babe Factor
Lunch
Bethlehem Steele
Stay Up

Music Producer
Album
No Peaking
Cliff Morrison
Co Producer/Artist
Son Of Jim Morrison

United Filmmakers, International
CFO
Co Producer
Twisted Nightmare
Demon Wind

Horowitz Management
President/CEO
Real Estate Developer
Student of Spirituality
2005-Present

Hormi Holding Company
President/CEO
Developer, Troy, New York
Real Estate
Initiated New York State 30 percent Film Tax Credit
New York State Senate Majority Leader,
Senator Joseph Bruno

Author
2015
Life At 70: Pedal To The Metal

Whitefish Schools, Whitefish, Montana
Substitute Teacher
Tutor
First Grade Thru 12Th Grade
Specialized With Special Need Students
2016-Present

About the Author

SANFORD (SANDY) J HOROWITZ

"Eclectic" is the most appropriate word that defines Sanford's life. After graduating college and serving in army intelligence during the Vietnam years, Sanford worked in New York City in management for a major manufacturer. Shortly after, an opportunity arose to supervise construction of a residential home in Port Antonio, Jamaica, W.I. where he spent 3 years. When he completed the project in 1971, Sanford was invited to Los Angeles. He stayed with his cousin who was married to Paul Hunt and Sanford became close friends. Paul was a young filmmaker and offered Sanford partnership in a new film venture, "United Filmmakers, Int." Together, they produced and distributed over a dozen films domestic and internationally. That was when Sandy travelled the world.

Made in the USA
Columbia, SC
26 September 2019